AMERICA

THEN & NOW

EDITED BY DAVID COHEN
TEXT BY SUSAN WELS

*This book was made possible by a generous grant from the Kmart Corporation
in celebration of its 30th anniversary*

PUBLISHED BY COHEN PUBLISHERS
MILL VALLEY, CALIFORNIA

AMERICA: THEN & NOW

Copyright ©1992 by Cohen Publishers, Inc. All rights reserved.

Printed in Hong Kong by Toppan Printing Co., Ltd. No part of this book may be used or reprinted in any manner

whatsoever without permission, except in the case of brief quotations embodied in critical articles and reviews.

For information, please write to: Cohen Publishers, Inc., 200 Alta Vista Avenue, Mill Valley, CA 94941.

FIRST EDITION

Library of Congress Cataloging-in-Publication Data

AMERICA: THEN & NOW/David Cohen, editor.—

1st ed.

      p. cm.

      ISBN: 0-9630960-0-1

      1. American history–Pictorial works. 2 Photography; artistic. I. Cohen, David 1955-

91-76989

92   93   94   95   T.P.   5   4   3   2   1

Frank A. Rinehart, Omaha, Nebraska, 1898

"The Mirror with a Memory"

Even in these days of hand-held video cameras, when almost anyone can make their own movies in living color, the still photograph has a special power. It is the capacity to capture a moment in time and preserve it forever. In a world that is changing ever more quickly, this is a precious power, indeed. Inside our own family albums, there is a wonderful place where mom and dad just got married, the cutest babies never grow up, grandma is still young and lovely, grandpa, forever strong and virile.

When we set out to rediscover America with old pictures and new, we had no idea of the treasure that would be set before us. All over the country, there are carefully tended collections of these frozen moments—magic places where history comes alive before your eyes.

In an appropriately dark and hushed room in the bowels of The New York Public Library, a young scholar will show you stereoscopic images made by Eadweard Muybridge, the peripatetic English photographer who travelled America in the last half of the 19th century. Muybridge and his colleagues captured the ebullient life and unspoiled wilderness of a young country on glass negatives and paper prints. And there in the library, preserved in long, dark oak drawers, is their world of ghosts—a land where handsome men wear spats and bowlers, beautiful women in long dresses push wicker baby carriages, and boys in knee pants play stickball on the clean streets of New York. Don't get too attached—even the children are long gone now—yet their images live on, immutable and alluring.

Denver, Colorado, 1866

A collection of these spectral vignettes drawn from the last 150 years of America's life and times would make a marvelous book on its own. But we kept asking ourselves the same question over and over: If we went back to the same places, tried to recapture the same scenes, what would it all look like now? And if these new scenes were juxtaposed with the old, what could we learn about the ebb and flow of life in America?

As it turned out, there was a lot to learn. Pioneers cut their sod houses from the hard dirt, because there was no wood to be had on the vast, treeless frontier. Morrison Remick Waite, the Chief Justice of the Supreme Court in 1876, had no judicial experience at all when President Ulysses S. Grant appointed him. The first automobile was not introduced to America by Henry Ford at the turn of the century. There was actually a self-propelled vehicle, the Orukter Amphibolos, on these shores as early as 1804. Ford just saw the potential. He didn't invent the car. He reinvented it—revolutionizing the way that society produced goods of all sorts in the process.

That was probably the best lesson we learned: that the 19th-century French commentator Alexis de Tocqueville was right. The genius of America is in its ability to continually reinvent itself, to bring men, women and children from all nations and make Americans of them, to use their vast potential to light a beacon for the world to follow. We haven't always been fair, nor have we always been right, but most of the time we Americans have been open to change. As you view the pictures in this book, we think you will find that much of the time, that change has been for the better.

4

Arthur Telfer, Cooperstown, New York, c.1885

This project would not have been possible without the assistance and support of many people. Foremost among these are Joseph Antonini, chairman, and Michael Wellman, vice-president of marketing of the Kmart Corporation. When they heard the idea, they liked it and commissioned this book to celebrate Kmart's 30th birthday. (A section discussing the history of Kmart over the past 30 years appears at the back of this book.) George Craig, the chairman of HarperCollins Publishers, was among the first to hear this notion. He immediately said, "We'll do it, " and an expanded hardcover version of this volume will be published by HarperCollins in the fall of 1992.

This book was put together by a fine staff that worked excessively hard to get it out on time. But the real stars of this show are, of course, the photographers—then and now. In the old days, photographers like Mathew Brady and William Henry Jackson would roam the country, using a marvelous new invention to show Americans their world—a contraption that Oliver Wendell Holmes called "the mirror with a memory."

To make this book, a talented group of modern photographers took to the road in jeeps and vans, retracing the steps of the itinerant photographers of old. If the old photographers set out to document the wonders of a brash, young country, this new group set out to rediscover the country as it is now. We hope that by reading this book, you too will be able to rediscover America. Maybe you can show your children and grandchildren what life was like back then and introduce them to our ghostly friends from the old days—those friends who never grow old.

—D.C.

Above, Washington, DC, c.1860; Right, Nick Kelsh, Washington, DC

When Congress decided to move the seat of government from Philadelphia to Washington, DC, in 1790, critics called the proposed site "a howling, malarious wilderness." But the government moved anyway, and in 1793, construction began on the U.S. Capitol building, a Palladian structure designed by a brilliant, young physician and amateur architect named William Thornton.

In 1814, the nearly completed Capitol was burned by British troops who set furniture, paintings, books and carpets ablaze. Reconstruction began the following year and wasn't finished until 1829.

In 1850, the construction of two new wings was halted during the Civil War when the Capitol was used as a barracks, bread bakery and military hospital. But in 1861, despite the pressing demands of the war, President Lincoln wanted construction to continue as a symbol of his faith in the Union. In 1863, after the building's nine-million-pound, cast-iron dome was completed, Thomas Crawford's *Freedom* was erected at its crown.

Mathew Brady, 1862

This Civil War trooper, with a pistol in his belt and unsheathed saber, was a member of the Union Army's 3rd Cavalry Regiment. The regiment fought Confederate troops in New Mexico before moving to Memphis, where it participated in nearly every major cavalry campaign for the rest of the war.

The average age of Civil War soldiers was 25, and one in four was foreign born. Very likely, this soldier wore a metal neck clamp which kept his head perfectly still while posing for this photograph—a three-minute exposure.

Shelly Katz, Fort Bliss, Texas

The U.S. Cavalry was officially "unhorsed" in 1942, and today, the 3rd Armored Cavalry Regiment is a tank and airborne unit stationed at Fort Bliss in El Paso, Texas.

Above, Specialist Cristobal De Jesus Vazquez, 26, wears desert camouflage, including a lightweight helmet, flashlight, first-aid kit and goggles. Vazquez carries an M16 automatic rifle that fires 30 rounds in 20 seconds. He recently returned from the Persian Gulf region, where the 3rd Cavalry captured three airfields, fought Iraq's Republican Guards in two major battles and suffered only one casualty.

Left, Grabill Studio, Pine Ridge, South Dakota, 1891; Above, Paul Chesley, Pine Ridge, South Dakota

On a cold, clear day in December 1890, the United States Seventh Cavalry opened fire on the Minnonconjou Sioux at Wounded Knee Creek near this Pine Ridge, South Dakota, village, left. As many as 200 Sioux, half of them women and children, lost their lives in the carnage.

The origin of the Wounded Knee massacre can be traced to the Ghost Dance cult, a spiritual movement that the Oglala Sioux adapted from a Paiute visionary. The desperate drought- and disease-ridden Sioux believed that performance of the Ghost Dance could bring about a messianic age when the living and dead would be reunited and the vast buffalo herds would return. Fearing that the charismatic power of this new religion would unite the Sioux, Arapaho and Cheyenne and inspire an uprising, General Nelson Miles of the Seventh Cavalry ordered the arrest of the Oglala Sioux leaders, including the elderly chief Sitting Bull, who was killed in the ensuing melee.

The cavalry then rounded up 350 Sioux and moved them to a camp at Wounded Knee Creek, where the federal troops attempted to disarm them. When a shot rang out, the cavalry opened fire, and even survivors were pursued and butchered. The Sioux surrendered a year later, ending, for the most part, the long and bloody conflicts between U.S. troops and Native Americans. Ironically, the 25 original ghost dancers were not killed and ended up touring Europe as part of Buffalo Bill Cody's Wild West Show.

Today, members of the Sioux nation still live on the Pine Ridge plains, above. In 1973, members of the American Indian Movement captured the village of Wounded Knee and challenged federal authorities to repeat the massacre. The activists held this symbolic ground for 72 days and lost two men before surrendering.

Solomon Butcher, East Custer County, Nebraska, 1887

With the lure of free land promised by the Homestead Act of 1862, thousands of East Coast settlers and immigrants from France, Germany and Scandinavia streamed into the harsh, treeless prairies of Nebraska. For most, the only material available for building homes was the land itself. Plows sliced up long strips of well-soaked earth, which were then chopped into bricks and formed into walls. Dull gray in the dry season, the cramped "soddies" bloomed with prairie roses, weeds and morning glories when the rains came.

Paul Chesley, Comstock, Nebraska

Philip Dowse, 84, still proudly tends the sod home his father built in Broken Bow, Nebraska, in 1900. One of the first sod houses built in Custer County, it is maintained as a museum and listed on the National Register for Historic Places. Dowse spent nine years restoring the house and still has the original plow his father used to cut his home from the prairie.

Clark Ensminger, Florida, 1890s

In the 1890s, millions of American children in rural regions were educated in one-room schoolhouses like this one, possibly in the Everglades, a sparsely settled marshland in southern Florida. Children of all sizes were taught by a single teacher, who was frequently paid in pork, corn, whiskey or other goods. There were nearly 200,000 one-room schoolhouses in America in 1917—accounting for 75 percent of all schools.

Henry Groskinsky, Miami, Florida

When school buses came into use, most states consolidated their small, rural, one-room schools into larger school districts. Only 640 one-room schoolhouses remain in America today.

In the 300,000-student Dade County, Florida, school district, students gather outside the new Majory Stoneman Douglas School, above. Opened in September 1991, the building has classrooms, labs and cafeteria facilities for 1,200 students from pre-kindergarten through fifth grade. The school was named for the 102-year-old "Everglades Evangelist," known for her tireless efforts to preserve the fragile environment and endangered species of the Everglades.

Above, Darius Kinsey, western Washington, c.1900
Right, Ed Lowe, Orting, Washington

The massive, old-growth trees of western Washington attracted settlers and ships throughout the last half of the 19th century. By 1905, the region's booming lumber industry was milling 3.5 billion board feet of lumber, more than any other state in the nation.

Early loggers cut down the huge trees with axes, and it was not until the 1870s that felling saws appeared. Even with the help of saws, however, it took logging crews like the one above a full day to bring down a single tree and cut it into lengths that could be hauled to the mill by oxen, horse or, later, locomotives.

Today, Washington lumbermen like Lee Hughes, Ray Cooper and Mike Winterringer can fell and cut a big tree in an hour with chain saws and powerful yarding machinery that lifts the timber onto trucks. Although many of Washington's old-growth trees have been cleared, replanting efforts begun in the 1940s are beginning to yield a second growth.

J.E. Stimson, New Castle, Wyoming, 1907

In the decades following the Civil War, many middle-class women turned their attention to self-improvement and community service. By the late 1880s, hundreds of women's civic, literary and athletic clubs had sprung up across the country.

The Owls, above, founded in 1894, comprised the first women's self-improvement group in Weston County, Wyoming. It was so named because its 16 members sought wisdom through the study and discussion of literature, art, music, history and religion.

Paul Chesley, Cheyenne, Wyoming

Today, members of the Women's Civic League of Cheyenne, Wyoming, concern themselves with community service instead of academic studies. The 340-member club usually decorates a local home at Christmas time, and proceeds from the sale of crafts and decorations are used for community improvements. Last year, the organization raised thousands of dollars for groups including foster grandparents and battered wives, and they helped fund health care for low-income women.

Left, New Haven, Connecticut, 1890; Above, Sebastian Frinzi, New Haven

In 1890, Yale's high-scoring football team, led by quarterback Frank Barbour (front row, far right), dominated rival squads, trouncing Wesleyan 76-0 and Rutgers 70-0. The team lost only one close game that year, a bruising 6-12 match against Harvard.

The team's coach was football legend Walter Camp, a Yale graduate considered to be the father of modern football. Under Camp's influence from 1884 to 1914, the modern game was organized, and the first all-America team was selected. Even in Camp's day, however, American football was more like a brutal cousin of British rugby than the sport that's played today. Players trained as wrestlers and boxers and competed without pads or helmets in grueling, 45-minute halves with no rests allowed. The sport was so punishing that Harvard cancelled its season in 1885.

Today, sports figures still pose by the venerable Yale Fence. Women, first admitted to the university in 1969, took up intercollegiate fencing in 1974 and scored national championships in 1981-82, 1983-84 and 1984-85 under coach Henry Harutunian. Senior Nicole Gray, above, a first-team, All-Ivy pick in 1991, captained the 1991-92 squad.

Above, Alice Austen, Annapolis, Maryland, September 25, 1894, 3:15 p.m.
Right, Nick Kelsh, Annapolis, Maryland

In 1894, above, midshipmen at the U.S. Naval Academy at Annapolis, Maryland, were drilled in boating on the Severn River. At the time, the school's 300 students learned both sailing and steam propulsion as part of their preparation for careers as naval officers. Annapolis's rigorous, four-year course of instruction was recognized by the Paris Exposition of 1878 as "the best system of education in the United States."

Today, the academy trains its 4,300 male and female midshipmen in nuclear power, astronautics and international politics, as well as seamanship and navigation. The rowboats are gone, but midshipmen, right, still train on the Severn River in 108-foot patrol vessels as part of their class work.

Left, Charles H. Currier, Boston, Massachusetts, 1890s; Above, Jean-Pierre Laffont, Boston, Massachusetts

Bicycling became an American mania in the 1890s, when enthusiasts traded in their dangerously unstable pennyfarthing bikes, left, for new "safety" bicycles, which had wheels of equal size. Although the Women's Rescue League warned that cycling threatened ladies' morals, women eagerly took up the sport. Some donned bloomers, while others kept their feet and ankles from view by weighing down their skirt hems with lead.

Bicycles were used for business as well as pleasure. Turn-of-the-century messengers carried mail, telegrams and parcels to businesses and homes, often along rutted dirt roads that jolted and sometimes toppled the rider. In 1907, United Parcel Service started as a foot- and bike-messenger business, and as late as 1940, most of Western Union's 20,000 uniformed couriers rode bikes.

Although their business was first dented by trolley cars and later by the invention of the fax machine, bike messengers still careen around Boston and most other major American cities, making deliveries to law firms, ad agencies and banks. Today's bike couriers, above, ride 10-speeds and mountain bikes. Their "uniforms" run to T-shirts, headphones and spandex pants.

Solomon Butcher, Cherry County, Nebraska, 1900

According to turn-of-the-century photographer Solomon Butcher, Miss Sadie Austin, above, was not only an accomplished musician, but the best-known cowgirl in Cherry County, Nebraska. "When her father was short of help," wrote Butcher, "Sadie...put on a divided skirt and rode the range."

Ranch women did everything, from cooking, cleaning and raising children to pitching hay and driving cattle. Many carried six-shooters—and some shamelessly traded in their divided skirts for denim britches which wouldn't flap and scare the horses.

Paul Chesley, Oshkosh, Nebraska

Today, in nearby Oshkosh, Nebraska, Jane McGinley, right, splits her time between schoolteaching at Oshkosh Elementary and helping her husband, Pete, herd and brand cattle on the 1,200-head Blue Creek Ranch. McGinley is no drugstore cowgirl. She competed in her first rodeo at the age of six and sometimes carries a shotgun to kill prairie rattlesnakes.

Left, C.E. Holmbor (?), Pueblo, Colorado, July 4, 1905; Above, Paul Chesley, near Denver, Colorado

Female daredevils were popular attractions in the early 1900s. Miss Eunice Padfield, left, performed a daring feat at the 1905 Colorado State Fair in Pueblo when she plummeted from a 35-foot platform to a pool below on the back of her horse, Silver King. Miss Padfield earned $150 for the jump, and both she and the horse survived unscathed.

Today, outside of Denver, daredevils of both sexes bungee-jump from a bridge 100 feet above a Rocky Mountain gorge. Here, Christine Warren from Adrenaline Adventures swan-dives from the bridge with 40-foot elasticized cords attached to her ankles. Asked why she chooses to leap from bridges, Warren told photographer Paul Chesley, "For the adrenaline rush."

Bungee-jumping, or something like it, was first performed in this country half a century ago by a man named The Great Peters, who tied an elasticized noose around his neck and swan-dived from a 75-foot rigging.

Above, William Henry Jackson, Chattanooga, Tennessee, probably 1892; Right, Torin Boyd, Chattanooga, Tennessee

Viewed from the slopes of Lookout Mountain in 1892, the town of Chattanooga, Tennessee, nestles gracefully in the S curves of the Tennessee River.

In 1838, Chattanooga was the starting point of the Trail of Tears—the brutal forced march of the Cherokee nation to Oklahoma under General Winfield Scott. Over a quarter of the 15,000 Cherokee died of disease and exposure during the journey. After the Cherokee were removed, the area was taken over by white settlers and became a transportation hub with the arrival of the steamboat in 1835 and the railroad in the 1840s.

The city was also the site of a series of Civil War engagements, including the Union victory at "The Battle above the Clouds" on Lookout Mountain. During that clash, Union General Ulysses S. Grant's troops struggled up the misty mountainside to victory against the Confederate soldiers who couldn't aim through the dense fog.

Today, Chattanooga, right, is still a busy transportation, industrial and commercial crossroads. Major changes in the landscape include the building of Interstate 24 along the river, lower right, in 1924.

Left, Catskill Mountains, New York, late 19th century; Above, Jean-Pierre Laffont, Arkville, New York

In the 1860s, New York's Catskill Mountains were a glamorous retreat for wealthy families seeking refuge from the summer heat. But when the railroads arrived in the 1870s, business really began to boom. Middle-class vacationers travelled northwest on rail lines like the Delaware and Ulster and flooded small hotels in Haines Falls and Tannersville. There, in 1902, a week's room and board could be had for $7. Wealthier families paid $35 a week at luxurious resorts like the Catskill Mountain House or the Hotel Kaaterskill.

Later, in the '40s and '50s, largely Jewish hotels like The Concord, Grossinger's and The Nevele became destinations for honeymoons and two-week vacations. Then, room rent included a private bath, huge, Kosher, all-you-can-eat meals and free shows by comedians like Sid Caesar, Buddy Hackett, Alan King and Jackie Mason.

Today, Catskill Mountain tourists, above, pay $7 to board a vintage Delaware and Ulster train for an hour-long excursion featuring a mock train robbery.

Left, J.P. Shafer, Morgantown, West Virginia, 1868; Above, Nick Kelsh, Morgantown, West Virginia

In the 1840s, Charles Ellet, Jr. took suspension bridge technology to the furthermost limits of the day when he built the world's longest suspension span across the Ohio River at Wheeling, West Virginia. (It later fell during a violent storm.) His encore to the Wheeling Bridge was a daring suspension bridge 250 feet above the roaring Niagara gorge. Ellet strung the first wire across the chasm on the string of a child's kite, and when a sideless roadway had been suspended, the publicity-minded engineer crossed the swaying, seven-foot-wide span on horseback.

An engineer named W. O. Buchanan, who had worked with Ellet on the Niagara span, built this classic suspension toll bridge, left, over the Monongahela River in Morgantown, West Virginia, in 1854. When it opened, the toll charges were "one cent per hog, three cents for pedestrian, 15 cents for a one-horse vehicle and 50 cents for a four-horse vehicle." Morgantown demolished the suspension bridge in 1907, and a new truss trolley bridge was built. In the 1980s, that span was replaced by a concrete and girder bridge with four lanes to carry modern highway traffic between Morgantown and Westover.

Charles H. Currier, Pumpkin Island, Maine, c.1890

Pumpkin Island Light in Maine's Penobscot Bay featured state-of-the-art optical technology when it opened in 1854. Its Fresnel lens, ground in Paris, used prisms to focus the light of an oil lamp into a powerful, concentrated beam.

A one-legged Civil War veteran named Charles Leroy Babson tended the lighthouse with his wife, Georgianna, and two sons from 1870 until 1902. Although lighthouse keepers were given a small salary and a dwelling for their labors, their lives were usually hard and lonely. Often isolated on rocky, barren islands, they were exposed to severe weather without benefit of neighbors, schools or even soil for raising food.

Jean-Pierre Laffont, Pumpkin Island, Maine

Automated in 1933 as a cost-saving measure during the Depression, the Pumpkin Island Light was officially deactivated in 1934, when it was purchased for $552 by Senator George Harmon of Bar Harbor. In 1946, the station was sold to the Alexander Stewart family, who tended it as a private residence for 45 years. By the late 1980s, all but one of the once-manned lighthouses in America were completely automated and outfitted with radio and radar beacons. The figure of the brave and lonely lighthouse keeper slipped into history.

Above, Wilhelm Hester, Port Blakely, Washington, 1905; Right, Ed Lowe, Seattle, Washington

When German immigrant Wilhelm Hester photographed these tall ships tied up at Port Blakely, Washington, in 1905, the mighty windjammers were already seeing their final days.

In remote Puget Sound, however, tall-masted lumber barks and schooners still loaded with lumber and grain and set sail for South America, Australia, Hawaii and Alaska. Hester made his early career in and around Port Blakely taking and selling photographs of sailing ships and sailors, who were the romantic heroes of their day. It was an exciting and difficult profession. In January, 1899 Hester photographed the crew of the bark *Andelana*, awaiting her cargo of wheat bound for England. Later that night, the ship capsized, and every man Hester photographed was lost.

Today, the Port of Seattle, right, is still an export center for lumber, as well as animal feed, aluminum, cotton and frozen vegetables—mostly bound for the Pacific Rim nations. At right, the South Korean ship *Hanjin Pohang* takes on her cargo of logs, lumber, cotton and hides, recyclable waste paper and scrap metal.

Left, photographer and location unknown, c.1900; Above, Jamie Thompson, Pasadena, California

Alexander Graham Bell patented the telephone in 1876 and formed the Bell Telephone Company the next year with just 778 telephones in service. Phone connections were made manually by operators in central switching offices. Emma M. Nutt, hired in 1878, was the first female Bell System employee. By the time she retired in 1915, women had almost completely replaced men at operator switchboards across the country.

Although the dial telephone was first invented in 1891 by a Kansas City undertaker named Almos B. Strowger, it did not come widely into use until the late 1940s. As homes and offices gradually converted to direct-dial technology, manual switchboards began to close. The last Bell System manual switchboard, on California's Santa Catalina Island, shut down in 1978.

Today, Bell System's 6,300 operators field requests for information and assistance from more than 155 million telephone customers in the United States. Male and female operators at the Pacific Bell exchange in Pasadena, California, each handle up to 1,100 requests a day for information. Americans now make more than 800 million phone calls every day.

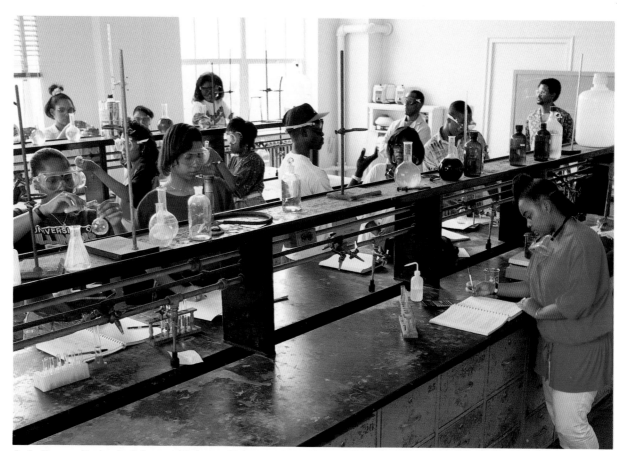

Left, Frances Benjamin Johnston, Tuskegee, Alabama, 1903; Above, Shelly Katz, Tuskegee, Alabama

Tuskegee Institute in central Alabama was founded in 1881 by Booker T. Washington, a former child slave who graduated from Virginia's Hampton Institute in 1872. Starting with a $2,000 appropriation from the Alabama State Legislature, Washington single-handedly taught 30 students in a tumbledown church and shack. Tuskegee was one of the first schools in the nation established to train black teachers. Washington believed that blacks could preserve their constitutional rights and improve their position in society only through hard work and education.

The experiment was a widely admired success. By 1896, Tuskegee Institute had blossomed into an institution with a student body of 300 and a staff of 35. The school's property included a large farm and academic buildings built by students.

That same year, Dr. George Washington Carver joined the faculty, and under his scientific leadership, Tuskegee became a pioneer in agricultural research. A former slave, Carver developed 300 new products from the peanut and 118 from the sweet potato.

Today, the school, now called Tuskegee University, occupies a 5,000-acre campus and educates some 3,700 undergraduates and graduate students. Undergrads like those above can earn degrees in agricultural specialties such as botany, animal sciences and agronomy, or in areas as diverse as aerospace engineering, chemistry, English, finance, psychology and early childhood education.

Left, Lewis W. Hine, New York, New York, c.1905; Above, Paul Chesley, Los Angeles, California

In 1904, more than 200,000 Italian immigrants boarded steamships for America. The poorest crossed the Atlantic in cramped, dirty steerage quarters. When they arrived in New York Harbor after nearly a month at sea, they underwent the processing ordeal at Ellis Island, the federal immigration station established in 1891. There they were examined, questioned, sometimes given new names, then admitted or refused. Those allowed to stay took the ferry to Manhattan, where they sought menial labor which still paid two to three times the wages they could earn in Italy.

Today, Los Angeles is second only to New York as the largest point of entry for new immigrants. Fifty-six thousand of the nation's 402,000 immigrants arrive in L. A. each year from 105 countries. In October 1991, Himawana Apiwibowo of Indonesia, above, landed at LAX with his wife, three sons and four carts of luggage. Like the teeming millions before them, they came to start a new life in America.

Born on the "Golden Triangle" where the Allegheny and Monongahela rivers meet to form the mighty Ohio, Pittsburgh, Pennsylvania, was already an industrial giant by the late 1800s. At that time, the city produced nearly all of the world's oil, half of its iron and glass and two-thirds of America's crucible steel.

But this titanic productivity had a cost. Pittsburgh became a sprawling, smoke-belching, industrial city with smog so thick that street lamps sometimes had to be lit by early afternoon. When asked in the 1940s how he would improve Pittsburgh, architect Frank Lloyd Wright declared, "Abandon it."

In the early 1980s, thousands did abandon Pittsburgh as the domestic steel industry contracted and some 90,000 heavy manufacturing jobs vanished. But the city has, in many ways, recreated itself. Pollution and flood controls cleared the air and reined in the once-sulfureous rivers. Slums were razed, and parks and corporate plazas were built. Today, Pittsburgh is replacing steelworking jobs with positions in high-technology, health, research and education. In 1985, Pittsburghers nodded knowingly when their hometown was rated "Most Livable City in the United States" by *Places Rated Almanac*.

Right, Pittsburgh, Pennsylvania, c.1905
Following pages, Nick Kelsh, Pittsburgh, Pennsylvania

Nick Kelsh, Kennett Square, Pennsylvania

Guillermo Beauchamp, 61, says that when he immigrated from Puerto Rico in 1952, he fulfilled his dream to follow his three sons to America. Beauchamp has picked mushrooms at Phillips' huge indoor mushroom farm in Kennett Square, Pennsylvania since 1987. Twenty percent of the farm's workers are from Puerto Rico, 75 percent are from Mexico. Workers on the farm earn up to $400 for a 50-hour week.

Born on the "Golden Triangle" where the Allegheny and Monongahela rivers meet to form the mighty Ohio, Pittsburgh, Pennsylvania, was already an industrial giant by the late 1800s. At that time, the city produced nearly all of the world's oil, half of its iron and glass and two-thirds of America's crucible steel.

But this titanic productivity had a cost. Pittsburgh became a sprawling, smoke-belching, industrial city with smog so thick that street lamps sometimes had to be lit by early afternoon. When asked in the 1940s how he would improve Pittsburgh, architect Frank Lloyd Wright declared, "Abandon it."

In the early 1980s, thousands did abandon Pittsburgh as the domestic steel industry contracted and some 90,000 heavy manufacturing jobs vanished. But the city has, in many ways, recreated itself. Pollution and flood controls cleared the air and reined in the once-sulfureous rivers. Slums were razed, and parks and corporate plazas were built. Today, Pittsburgh is replacing steelworking jobs with positions in high-technology, health, research and education. In 1985, Pittsburghers nodded knowingly when their hometown was rated "Most Livable City in the United States" by *Places Rated Almanac*.

Right, Pittsburgh, Pennsylvania, c.1905
Following pages, Nick Kelsh, Pittsburgh, Pennsylvania

Left, Lewis W. Hine, New York, New York, c.1905; Above, Paul Chesley, Los Angeles, California

In 1904, more than 200,000 Italian immigrants boarded steamships for America. The poorest crossed the Atlantic in cramped, dirty steerage quarters. When they arrived in New York Harbor after nearly a month at sea, they underwent the processing ordeal at Ellis Island, the federal immigration station established in 1891. There they were examined, questioned, sometimes given new names, then admitted or refused. Those allowed to stay took the ferry to Manhattan, where they sought menial labor which still paid two to three times the wages they could earn in Italy.

Today, Los Angeles is second only to New York as the largest point of entry for new immigrants. Fifty-six thousand of the nation's 402,000 immigrants arrive in L. A. each year from 105 countries. In October 1991, Himawana Apiwibowo of Indonesia, above, landed at LAX with his wife, three sons and four carts of luggage. Like the teeming millions before them, they came to start a new life in America.

Lewis W. Hine, Pennsylvania, 1909

In 1909, Lewis W. Hine photographed this Polish track layer working the grim coal fields of Pennsylvania. Thousands of the 13 million Poles, Hungarians and other immigrants who came to America from 1900 to 1914 sought employment in the mines and mills. If they were lucky enough to get the work, they hacked, blasted and shoveled black coal from dawn until dark, earning their pay by the 3,360-pound "miner's ton." Miners of this era often toiled 12 hours a day, seven days a week, to earn their dollar a day.

Left, eastern Washington, c.1900; Above, Ed Lowe, Colville, Washington

Until the early 1900s, many farmers depended, literally, on "horsepower" to plow, cultivate, mow, rake and reap their crops. These Holt sidehill combined harvesters, left, pulled by as many as 40 horses, were designed for harvesting the large, hilly acreage of West Coast farms.

Labor-saving devices like the sidehill allowed the average farmer to plant and harvest more than 250 acres of wheat per year in 1890, compared to only 15 acres in 1830. Still, horse-drawn machinery had its drawbacks. If one horse was stung by a bee and bolted, the rest of the animals could stampede and ruin the combine by stripping its gears.

By 1900, horse-pulled harvesters were replaced by self-propelled machines. Dee Terry, above, a 74-year-old wheat farmer in Colville, Washington, north of Spokane, can harvest up to 50 acres a day in his $105,000 air-conditioned New Holland TR95 harvester. Terry and his sons, Dale and Dan, harvest more wheat in a year than Washington's pioneer farmers could reap in a lifetime.

Orlando K. Parker, near Yosemite Valley, California, 1913

In 1878, two woodsmen from Vermont named James and David Lumsden sawed and blasted a huge hole through the trunk of a 50-foot-tall redwood stump called the "Dead Giant." They thought it would make a great attraction for stagecoach tourists sightseeing in California's Yosemite Valley. For better or worse, plans to carve a refreshment stand on one side of the huge stump never materialized. But stagecoach passengers did get the thrill of careening down a hill through the 10-foot-wide gap, with just a foot of headroom and inches to spare on each side. When sightseeing by stagecoach was replaced by automobile touring around 1913, the drive-through stump remained a popular attraction.

Alice Patterson, near Yosemite National Park, California

Today, tourists like Kevin, Susanne and Kendall Joyce and their friends can still drive through the Dead Giant on a one-way road leading from Crane Flat to Big Oak Flat, 10 miles north of Yosemite National Park. The tree is one of only two tunnel trees remaining near the park, and the only one that the public can still drive through. The 230-foot-tall California Tree, carved in 1895, is now off-limits, and Yosemite's world-famous, 2,100-year-old Wawona Tunnel Tree, carved in 1881, was sadly toppled by a heavy snowfall in 1969.

Left, Speedway, Indiana, 1911; Above, Ron McQueeney, Speedway, Indiana

The first major motor race at Indianapolis was a 300-mile contest held in 1909. The dirt and gravel track didn't hold up, and two years later, the Indianapolis 500, left, was inaugurated on a new track made of 3.2 million bricks. That year, Ray Harroun streaked to the finish line in a Marmon Wasp averaging 74 miles per hour.

"The Brickyard," as Indianapolis Speedway came to be known, is now the world's oldest surviving auto racetrack, and although the original bricks were paved over with asphalt in 1961, they can still be seen at the starting line.

Over the years, the course has served as a laboratory for the American automobile industry. Innovations such as four-wheel brakes were first tested on its 2.5-mile, rectangular course. It is also the sporting world's best-attended annual event, regularly drawing over 300,000 spectators. In 1991, Rick Mears won the Indy in a Marlboro Penske Chevy, clocking an average speed of more than 176 miles per hour.

Left, Boston, Massachusetts, 1903; Above, Joe Rossi, Minneapolis, Minnesota

On October 13, 1903, the Boston Americans whipped the Pittsburgh Nationals, 3-0, in the final game of the first World Series, held at Boston's Huntington Avenue Ball Field, left.

Boston, the champions of the upstart, three-year-old American League, took the Series from the venerable National League winners in a five-to-three game upset.

Contrary to popular belief, baseball was probably not invented by Abner Doubleday in Cooperstown, New York, in 1839. Early forms of the game, evolved from cricket and rounders, were already popular by the 1820s. A better candidate for the father of modern baseball would be a New York City bank teller and volunteer fireman named Alexander Cartwright. His team, the Knickerbocker Baseball Club, first played the game with flat clubs and a catgut-and-parchment ball in a Manhattan park, where they established the nine-player team and four-base diamond. Later, the rules were amended to limit the game to nine innings. Previously the winner had been the first team to score 21 runs.

In 1991, above, the Minnesota Twins prevented baseball's first Canadian-American World Series by trouncing the Toronto Blue Jays in the American League play-offs. The Twins, playing in the Hubert H. Humphrey Metrodome, went on to take the World Series from the Atlanta Braves. Minnesota's highest-paid player, center fielder Kirby Puckett, earned $3.3 million for the 1991 season. The average salary paid to players on the 1903 Americans was $3,000.

Virgil G. Jackson, Leadville, Colorado, c.1885

In the 1880s, Leadville, Colorado, was a prosperous, lusty mining town that knew how to have fun. Leadville boasted 23 restaurants, four banks and 97 saloons. In those days, rowdy customers would call for beer, whisky and mixed drinks such as Buffalo Bill Cody's favorite, the Stone Fence (a shot of rye poured in a glass of cider, topped with a lemon twist).

By necessity, Leadville's pioneer bartenders had to shoot as well as pour. Their customers included Old Man Beebe, who "killed three bartenders and crippled two." Old Man Beebe also killed the bartender who made that observation.

Paul Chesley, Leadville, Colorado

Today, Leadville's 113-year-old Silver Dollar Saloon still stands with its original bar, musk ox heads, spitoons and swinging doors. Owner Patricia Ann McMahon, center, bought the saloon 30 years ago and runs it with manager Carrol Nelson, second from the right. Most of the customers these days are tourists and locals employed at the area's ski resorts. The most popular mixed drinks at the Silver Dollar include Hot Chocolate Schnapps, Margaritas and Irish Coffee.

H.A. Abercromby, Pottstown, Pennsylvania, 1900

In 1880, Pottstown, Pennsylvania, was afflicted by drunken roughs, rollicking party girls and rowdy mill workers who poured into town to work in the booming iron industry. Like many smaller American towns of its time, Pottstown had no police force.

An editorial in a January 1880 issue of the *Montgomery Ledger* implored authorities to establish law and order, but it was three more years before $1,000 was budgeted for police protection. The constables who posed above in 1898 were known as "The Davidheiser Force," after Reuben Davidheiser, Chief Burgess of the borough.

Nick Kelsh, Pottstown, Pennsylvania

Since 1898, Pottstown has grown, and its 42 police officers have a budget of $2.6 million to handle the full range of modern urban ills, from petty theft to drug violations and homicides. Pottstown is no longer a boom town, however. In the 1980s, the city lost major industrial employers like Bethlehem Steel and Firestone. Now, Mrs. Smith's Pie Company provides a host of jobs (especially at pumpkin time), and small businesses fill the area's new industrial parks. Visitors to Pottstown can recall the heady turn-of-the-century days by strolling among the gas lamps, hitching posts and brick walks of the city's revitalized downtown area.

Left, Washington, DC, 1876; Above, National Geographic Society, Washington, DC

The Supreme Court began with only six justices in 1789 and had as many as ten between 1863 and 1866. It assumed its now-traditional, nine-member composition in 1869. In 1876, left, the Court was led by Chief Justice Morrison Remick Waite, center, a little-known railroad attorney from Ohio who had no judicial experience before President Grant nominated him as Chief Justice in 1873. Under Waite, the Court unanimously ruled that states could constitutionally bar both women and blacks from voting.

In 1991, the Supreme Court under Chief Justice William Hubbs Rehnquist has once again taken a conservative tack (by modern standards), reversing the liberal pronouncements of the Warren Court in the 1950s and '60s. Justice Thurgood Marshall, the first African-American member of the Supreme Court, retired in October 1991 after a quarter century on the bench. Conservative black justice Clarence Thomas (not pictured) was confirmed by the Senate that same month in a series of raucous hearings that riveted the nation with charges of sexual harassment.

Left, Lewis W. Hine, South Pittston, Pennsylvania, 1911; Above, Nick Kelsh, South Pittston, Pennsylvania

In 1911, photographer Lewis W. Hine documented the plight of the more than 1.5 million child laborers in the coal fields of eastern Pennsylvania. There, "breaker boys" as young as ten or twelve worked from seven in the morning until after dark every day of the week, separating lumps of coal from slate. Bundled in ragged coats and scarves, they sat at the picking tables, covered in black grime, as tons of rock tumbled in a deafening, dusty roar down chutes into their little breaker room. While older boys could earn up to $3 a week, a week's wage for the youngest was only a dollar.

Many coal companies employed breaker boys until the 1920s, when labor laws changed and new sorting machines were developed. Nowadays, impurities are removed by equipment coordinated by sophisticated computer systems controlled by just one person, such as Joseph Zieglar, above, at Consolidated Coal.

Above, Lewis W. Hine, St. Louis, Missouri, 1910
Right, Nick Kelsh, Philadelphia, Pennsylvania

Thanks to the wildly popular novels of Horatio Alger, the turn-of-the-century newsboy became a rags-to-riches symbol of hard work and thrift.

In reality, the life of the young street vendors was not nearly so romantic. Until the end of the 19th century, many were homeless orphans living in the squalid alleys behind printing plants. Others were the children of destitute families who sold papers for a penny apiece to help put food on the table.

"Little Fattie," above, was six years old and had already been selling papers for a year when Lewis W. Hine photographed him in St. Louis in 1910. Hine, a sociologist by trade, never intended his work to be artistic. He photographed the plight of child laborers in order to support a campaign to improve child labor laws.

Today, most newsboys have been replaced by vending machines and adult sellers, but in many communities, home delivery still falls to industrious school-age boys and girls. Thirteen-year-old Joey Baldino, right, delivers the *Philadelphia Daily News* to 26 South Philadelphia homes every afternoon when he comes home from school.

Above, Highland Park, Michigan, 1913; Right, Dana Fineman, Dearborn, Michigan

Although the first horseless carriage—an amphibious, steam-driven dredging machine called the Orukter Amphibolos—appeared in America as early as 1804, the car craze really took off in the 1890s when the Duryea "buggyaut" and Henry Ford's "quadricycle" became newfangled toys for the wealthy.

Ford knew he was onto something bigger than a rich man's plaything, however. In 1908, he introduced the Model T, a reliable, 20-horsepower contraption that rattled along at more than 25 miles per hour and was so simple it could be patched up with hairpins and chewing gum. By 1909, Ford had produced almost 18,000 "Tin Lizzies," at $850 apiece.

To meet soaring demand, Ford designed the first large-scale assembly line at his plant in Highland Park, Michigan, in 1913, above. Literally hundreds of concerns were producing cars at the time, but Ford's development of the assembly line and other mass-production techniques not only secured his company's future, but also revolutionized the way society produced goods of all sorts.

By 1913, 1,000 Ford car bodies a day were dropping down chutes onto waiting chassis. The time needed to assemble a car had dropped from 13 man-hours to six, and the price of a Model T (available in "any color," Ford said, "so long as it's black") had fallen to $440 by 1914 and $290 by 1924.

Today, the assembly line at the Ford plant in Wayne, Michigan, right, is manned by 325 robots that perform brazing operations and nearly 100 percent of the body welds on 1992 Ford Escorts. Overhead monorails later carry car bodies past human workers who install engines, electrical systems and trim.

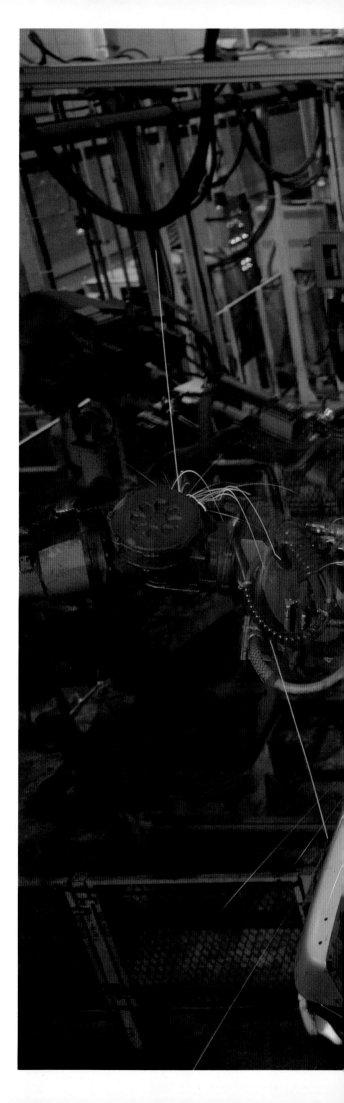

Probably Redington, Pennsylvania, c.1918

To help keep the troops supplied with artillery shells during World War I, the Bethlehem Steel Company opened a munitions plant in Redington, Pennsylvania, just east of the company's Bethlehem headquarters. A major supplier of cannons since the 1890s, Bethlehem Steel trained its Redington employees in the manufacture of explosives, shells and bombs. After the armistice in 1918, the plant converted to production of marine motors, hoists, oil burners and valves.

Nick Kelsh, Scranton, Pennsylvania

Today, civilian workers at the Army Ammunition Plant in Scranton, Pennsylvania, build M107 shells, which will later be fitted with explosives at another plant. These projectiles, designed to travel 10 to 14 miles and destroy tanks or buildings upon impact, were used in the United States' 1991 conflict with Iraq. The Scranton plant also produces state-of-the-art M864 rounds, which scatter multiple explosive devices over a wide area.

Left, U.S. Army Air Force, San Francisco, California, 1911
Above, Alice Patterson, Castle AFB, Merced, California

In January 1911, Lieutenant Myron Sidney Crissey of the Coast Artillery Corps, left, tested the first successful explosive aerial bomb. Crissey designed the 36-pound explosive which he adapted from an artillery shell, then dropped it from a Wright Model B biplane piloted by Phillip Parmelee during a trial run near San Francisco. The first use of aerial bombs in warfare was a primitive affair. Early World War I aircraft carried a passenger who simply pitched the bombs over the side. By 1915, German zeppelins carrying two tons of bombs were raining terror on Britain, and by the end of the war, 1,000-pound bombs were dropped by multi-engine bombers.

Today, at Castle Air Force Base in Merced, California, above, Captain Jim Bowles, Captain Ken Ariolo, Capain Mark Dibrelli, Captain Glenn Carlson and Captain Charlie Woodrow are pictured in front of a massive, eight-engine B-52G Stratofortress aircraft. First flown in 1954, B-52s still comprise the nation's primary manned strategic bomber force. With a range of more than 10,000 miles and a ceiling of 50,000 feet, B52Gs can carry 70,000 pounds of attack missiles, air-launched cruise and anti-ship missiles.

75

J.E. Stimson, Cheyenne, Wyoming, May 29, 1918

Soon after the United States entered World War I, 1.4 million women poured into the work force to replace the boys who went "over there." The women took jobs ranging from steeplejacking to mending railroad ties. These laborers at the Union Pacific Railroad's Cheyenne, Wyoming, freight yards did their gritty boilermaking, pipe-fitting and freight-handling jobs in coveralls, while their eastern counterparts labored in more "ladylike" aprons and ankle-length skirts. Although welcomed in the rail yards during wartime, most women lost their jobs when the war ended and the men came home.

Paul Chesley, Cheyenne, Wyoming

Today, women make up a small but growing percentage of Union Pacific's train workers. These engineers, yard foremen, brakemen, switchmen and conductors at the Cheyenne freight yard no longer have to shovel coal into boilers, but many of their tasks remain surprisingly similar to those performed by their counterparts in 1918.

Above, Washington, DC, c.1920; Right, Nick Kelsh, Washington, DC

In 1848, early feminists gathered at the first Women's Rights Convention in Seneca Falls, New York, to hear Elizabeth Cady Stanton, mother of seven, read a "Declaration of Sentiments" asserting that "all men and women are created equal."

Originally linked to the temperance and anti-slavery efforts, the campaign for women's suffrage made slow progress through the early 1900s. Before 1912, only six western states—Wyoming, Colorado, Utah, Idaho, Washington and California—had granted women the right to vote.

During the next eight years, however, Alice Paul's National Women's Party, headquartered in Washington, DC, above, mobilized a fourth generation of suffragists into militant picket lines, parades and noisy demonstrations. The political tide began to turn. In 1920, the 19th Amendment was ratified, and the female half of the U.S. population had won the right to vote.

Today, the headquarters of the National Organization for Women, right, is a center for feminist activity in the nation's capital. Led by Patricia Ireland (holding the flag), NOW mobilizes its quarter million members in 750 local and state chapters around issues from reproductive rights and the Equal Rights Amendment to protecting the rights of homemakers, lesbians, gays and older women.

Left, Memphis, Tennessee, 1917; Above, Torin Boyd, Memphis, Tennessee

Memphis entrepreneur Clarence Saunders revolutionized the grocery industry when he opened the first self-service market, left, in 1916.

Until that time, shoppers presented their grocery lists to clerks, who picked and packed the items from shelves, bins or barrels. Saunders' newfangled Memphis market saved labor costs for store owners and time for consumers. Although his fellow grocers predicted the idea would fail, consumers loved it. By 1918, hundreds of his Piggly Wiggly franchises had opened throughout the South and Midwest.

As to why the stores were called "Piggly Wiggly," one theory has it that Clarence Saunders was referring to the old nursery rhyme that begins, "This little piggy went to market." Saunders himself answered the question cryptically: "I named it that so people would ask me."

Today, Piggly Wiggly is a multi-billion-dollar franchise business, with more than 800 stores in 20 states, mostly in the Southeast. This 68,000-square-foot store, one of 10 in Memphis, serves more than 20,000 customers a week, 24 hours a day. High-speed checkout counters scan credit cards and bar codes, and customers can fax or phone in orders for delivery. In addition to 1,800 feet of self-service aisles, the store features an in-house florist, deli, video rental store and drive-through bank.

Left, Frank Cundill, Lantry, South Dakota, 1915; Above, Paul Chesley, Lantry, South Dakota

John "Hubert" McDaniel, left, was a year old when his bath was interrupted in 1915 by local prairie photographer Frank Cundill. McDaniel was born in this sod house in Lantry, South Dakota, which was built as a homestead by his father and grandfather. Pioneer life was rough on the northern plains, and the McDaniels had few furnishings— even their carpet was made from the tent the family lived in before the house was built.

As the small settlement at Lantry grew, the McDaniels operated a general store and post office out of the house. Hubert's grandmother, Carrie, became the town's first postmaster.

Today, Hubert is retired in Arvada, Colorado. His grandnephew, David, and his wife, Tammy, live in a house a few feet from where the original sod house once stood. Hubert's year-old grandniece, Minda, from Mitchell, South Dakota, reluctantly poses in the washtub, above, surrounded by a neighbor's pigs. In the background is the McDaniels' crop duster.

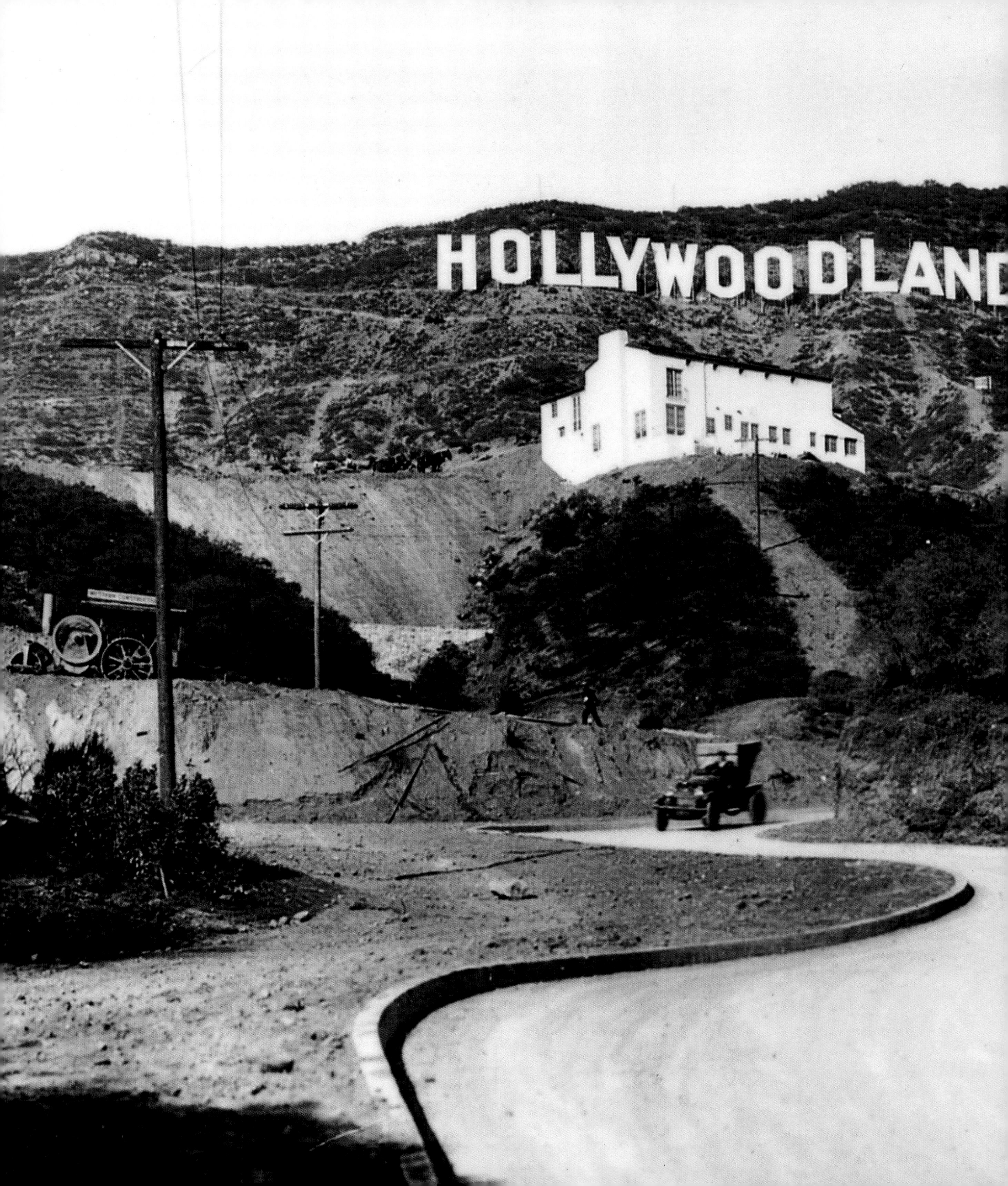
HOLLYWOODLAND

Left, Hollywood, California, c.1923; Above, Jamie Thompson, Hollywood, California

It was erected as a marketing gimmick to sell homes in the Hollywoodland subdivision of north Los Angeles in 1923 and shortened to read just "Hollywood" in 1949. But by the time the world-famous Hollywood sign was declared an historical cultural monument in 1973, it had suffered from years of neglect and disrepair and had to be completely replaced. Playboy mogul Hugh Hefner hosted a star-studded fund raising party to rebuild the sign, after rock star Alice Cooper donated $28,000 to replace the last "O" (in memory, he said, of Groucho Marx). Construction of the new 45-foot-high, steel-and-sheet-metal sign was completed in November 1978, once again marking the legendary capital of American movie making.

Above, Hollywood, California, 1916; Right, Paul Chesley, Hollywood, California

Inspired by a lecture given by photographer and motion studies pioneer Eadweard Muybridge, Thomas Edison patented the movie camera in 1887. The gadget didn't actually work at the time, and when it did, Edison decided against projecting films to audiences. He thought movies would have limited public appeal, and instead developed the kinetoscope to show short films to one person at a time.

Within twenty years, however, millions of Americans were crowding small storefront theaters, called nickelodeons, where 200 viewers at a time could watch a series of six or more silent, 10-minute comedy, adventure, melodrama and documentary films. Silent movie studios sprung up and began producing films for the new theater chains. (Each, in turn, was sued for patent infringement by Edison.)

One of the first silent movie companies was Vitagraph, which cranked out 300 short films a year by 1913. The filming of an anonymous Vitagraph production is shown above. The set had to be built outdoors because motion picture film of the time was not very sensitive to light.

Vitagraph became known for its immensely popular but undistinguished comedies, murder mysteries, romances and action films. Movies such as *Captain Swift* and *The Broadway Bubble* featured movie sirens like Alice Joyce and debonair leading men like Harry Morey.

Vitagraph was purchased in 1925 by Warner Brothers for $735,000. Its Hollywood studio is now the site of the ABC Television Center, home of the popular TV show "America's Funniest Home Videos," right. Like the Vitagraph studios it replaced, the show became successful because of new technology—small, relatively inexpensive video cameras that allow almost anyone to make short movies and send them in to "America's Funniest Home Videos" to compete for prizes.

Sculpted with pneumatic drills and dynamite, the Mount Rushmore National Memorial was created by the colorful and fiercely independent John Gutzon de la Mothe Borglum in the Black Hills of South Dakota.

Idaho-born Borglum studied art in Paris and was influenced by his friend, the celebrated French sculptor Auguste Rodin. Borglum's first attempt at a colossal sculpture—a depiction of Confederate heroes Jefferson Davis, Robert E. Lee and Stonewall Jackson at Stone Mountain, Georgia—was a bust. Borglum worked nine years on the project, then quit after a financial dispute with his sponsors.

Two years later, in 1927, Borglum accepted a commission from the federal government to build Mount Rushmore. He boldly predicted that the sculpture would take five years to complete. But the project took 14 years and was not concluded until shortly after Borglum's death in 1941.

The dimensions of the sculpture are truly monumental: Stretching 185 feet across, the faces of presidents George Washington, Thomas Jefferson, Abraham Lincoln and Theodore Roosevelt (representing the founding, philosophy, unity and expansion of America) are each 60 feet high.

In 1934, Jefferson was positioned on Washington's left, but the face later had to be blasted away and put next to Teddy Roosevelt when a large fissure developed in the granite. (See following page.) Borglum also blasted a tunnel into the rock well behind the faces which he hoped would house the U.S. Constitution, the Declaration of Independence and other important documents. These papers were never actually moved from their home at the National Archives in Washington DC, but the solid rock hallway still exists.

Left, Rapid City, South Dakota, c.1930
Following pages, Paul Chesley, Rapid City, South Dakota

Left, W.D. Smithers, Marfa, Texas, 1920s; Above, Shelly Katz, Dallas, Texas

The Temperance movement was a popular grassroots struggle for almost a century before it became a victim of its own success. In 1919, bowing to pressure from groups such as the Women's Christian Temperance League, Congress passed the 18th Amendment and the Volstead Act banning the manufacture, sale and consumption of alcoholic beverages.

Almost immediately, public consumption of spirits soared. New York's 15,000 legal pubs were replaced by 32,000 illegal speakeasies, and boozy "blind pigs" and "shock houses" flourished in even the driest Midwestern towns. The level of hypocrisy was dizzying: a 130-gallon-a-day whiskey still was discovered on the farm of the 18th Amendment's author, Senator Morris Sheppard. A jury trying a Prohibition case in San Francisco was found drunk on the evidence.

Organized crime moved in and corruption flourished. Even honest agents had their hands full trying to stem the torrential flow of alcohol smuggled in from Canada, the Caribbean and Mexico, left, in airplanes, ships and the secret compartments of souped-up motorcars.

Today, the same methods, and many more, are used to carry smuggled heroin, cocaine, marijuana and other illegal drugs into the United States. "If you can imagine a way to smuggle drugs, we've seen it, from dirty diapers to ice cream cones," says Dallas-based Drug Enforcement Agent Phil Jordan, above.

Above, New York, New York, c.1931; Right, Douglas Kirkland, New York, New York

When it was first thrust skyward in 1931, New York's 1,250-foot Empire State Building surpassed the Chrysler Building as the world's tallest skyscraper, a distinction it would hold for 40 years.

The builders of the Empire State Building were victims of bad timing. They broke ground on the site of the old Waldorf Astoria Hotel just three weeks before the great stock market crash of 1929. And although the building was rushed to completion in less than 18 months and came in under budget, by the time of the grand opening, the Great Depression was on, and most of the Empire State Building's 102 floors were unrented. Fortunately, the skyscraper was immediately world-famous, and the owners depended on admission fees from sightseers to help pay their taxes.

Over the years, America's archetypal skyscraper has worn two different caps. The first, above, was a domed mooring mast for dirigibles. Later, in 1950, a 222-foot television tower was added, giving the building its distinctive, spired look, right.

Douglas Kirkland, New York, New York

In February 1992, Tracy Allen Clark became a bride at St. John the Divine church on Manhattan's 116th Street. An actress, Tracy says many of her friends in the visual and performing arts are moving back to Harlem from Greenwich Village because of lower rents and increasing cultural activity. Harlem Week, held every August since 1975, celebrates the neighborhood's growing interest in home-grown music, theater and arts activities.

Above, New York, New York, c.1931; Right, Douglas Kirkland, New York, New York

When it was first thrust skyward in 1931, New York's 1,250-foot Empire State Building surpassed the Chrysler Building as the world's tallest skyscraper, a distinction it would hold for 40 years.

The builders of the Empire State Building were victims of bad timing. They broke ground on the site of the old Waldorf Astoria Hotel just three weeks before the great stock market crash of 1929. And although the building was rushed to completion in less than 18 months and came in under budget, by the time of the grand opening, the Great Depression was on, and most of the Empire State Building's 102 floors were unrented. Fortunately, the skyscraper was immediately world-famous, and the owners depended on admission fees from sightseers to help pay their taxes.

Over the years, America's archetypal skyscraper has worn two different caps. The first, above, was a domed mooring mast for dirigibles. Later, in 1950, a 222-foot television tower was added, giving the building its distinctive, spired look, right.

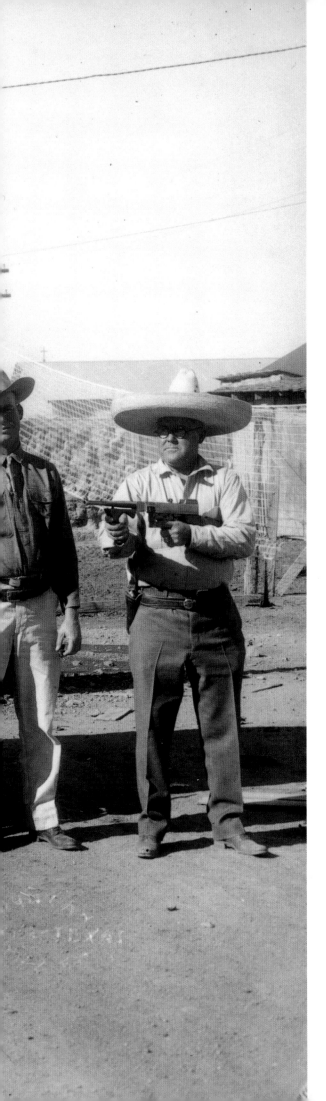

Left, W.D. Smithers, Marfa, Texas, 1920s; Above, Shelly Katz, Dallas, Texas

The Temperance movement was a popular grassroots struggle for almost a century before it became a victim of its own success. In 1919, bowing to pressure from groups such as the Women's Christian Temperance League, Congress passed the 18th Amendment and the Volstead Act banning the manufacture, sale and consumption of alcoholic beverages.

Almost immediately, public consumption of spirits soared. New York's 15,000 legal pubs were replaced by 32,000 illegal speakeasies, and boozy "blind pigs" and "shock houses" flourished in even the driest Midwestern towns. The level of hypocrisy was dizzying: a 130-gallon-a-day whiskey still was discovered on the farm of the 18th Amendment's author, Senator Morris Sheppard. A jury trying a Prohibition case in San Francisco was found drunk on the evidence.

Organized crime moved in and corruption flourished. Even honest agents had their hands full trying to stem the torrential flow of alcohol smuggled in from Canada, the Caribbean and Mexico, left, in airplanes, ships and the secret compartments of souped-up motorcars.

Today, the same methods, and many more, are used to carry smuggled heroin, cocaine, marijuana and other illegal drugs into the United States. "If you can imagine a way to smuggle drugs, we've seen it, from dirty diapers to ice cream cones," says Dallas-based Drug Enforcement Agent Phil Jordan, above.

93

James Van Der Zee, New York, New York, c.1930

From 1916 through the 1920s, photographer James Van Der Zee documented parades, weddings, street scenes and almost every aspect of life during the brilliant Harlem Renaissance—a period that saw a flowering of music, literature and theater in New York's black community.

The Harlem Renaissance gave rise to a literary movement that included writers like James Weldon Johnson, Langston Hughes, Countee Cullen and Rudolph Fisher. Harlem theaters like the Lafayette staged immensely popular musicals including *Shuffle Along* which catapulted Josephine Baker to fame. Dramas like Garland Anderson's *Appearances* started in Harlem and then moved downtown to the Broadway stage.

Above, Chicago, Illinois, 1940; Right, Dana Fineman, Chicago, Illinois

In the first decades of the twentieth century, Chicago was at the crux of the American railroad system. Grain and meat from the stockyards rolled out on rails to almost every corner of the country. And with more passenger terminals than any other American city, Chicago was the connecting point for travelers on the Illinois Central, Topeka & Santa Fe, Rock Island, New York Central, Alton, Chicago & Northwestern and other great railway lines. Movie stars, celebrities and other well-heeled passengers enjoyed the comforts of a first-class hotel aboard luxury expresses like the *Broadway Limited* to New York, which was staffed with maids and manicurists. The *Empire Builder* treated guests to reading cars, afternoon tea and a nightcap before bed.

The golden age of the American railroad began after the Civil War. New rail lines opened up the American frontier for many and built great fortunes for a few. Less than a century later, when the picture above was taken, the handwriting was already on the wall. Private automobiles, buses, airplanes and trucks were capturing a growing share of the nation's passenger and freight traffic. These modes of transport were less regulated and better subsidized by the government, and by the 1970s, ten midwestern and northeastern railroads had fallen into bankruptcy. The entire industry began a period of restructuring and consolidation.

In 1971, 18 of the 22 largest passenger railroads joined the government-operated Amtrak system that now carries nearly all intercity passengers. Several of the great Chicago passenger lines to the suburbs are now operated by Metra, Chicago's commuter rail system that fans out to Joliet, Aurora, Big Timber, Harbor, Zion and Fox Lake. Metra carries 70 million passengers a year on 1,200 miles of track stretching east into Indiana and north to Wisconsin.

Charles Hiller, San Francisco, California, October 1936

When it was completed in 1937, San Francisco's Golden Gate Bridge was the longest suspension span in the world. Its mammoth 65-story center towers support a roadway 4,200 feet long above a treacherous strait linking the Pacific Ocean and San Francisco Bay. The Golden Gate's 36.5-inch-diameter cables are still the largest bridge cables ever made, containing enough wire to circle the earth more than three times at the equator.

Workers under the direction of the brilliant Joseph Strauss braved earthquakes, ice and frighteningly precarious wind conditions to build the bridge. During construction, nine workers were saved by a huge safety net, earning them membership in the "Halfway to Hell" club. Ten others were not so lucky; they fell through the net into the icy waters.

Alice Patterson, San Francisco, California

Today, hundreds of tourists on foot and more than 120,000 vehicles cross the Golden Gate Bridge each day. Modern day commuters coping with bridge traffic would be distressed to know that only 25 vehicles a day crossed the Golden Gate in its first year of operation. No bridge on earth is more exposed to the elements—from the near-daily salt, rain and fog to winds that occasionally reach 60 miles per hour. To protect the bridge's 10 million square feet of steel, it is always being painted. By the time painters finish one coat of orange-vermillion (which takes four years), it's time to begin again at the other end.

Left, T.P. Robinson, Winter Park, Florida, 1930s; Above, Torin Boyd, Winter Park, Florida

Florida became East Coast America's winter playground in the 1920s, when middle-class tourists began driving their new automobiles down by the thousands. Speculators soon followed, cashing in on a frenzied but short-lived land boom. A lot of the tourists ended up staying, and from 1920 to 1930 the state's population increased by over 50 percent to nearly 1.5 million inhabitants. Florida's position as a tourist and retirement haven was established.

This 1938 photo advertised Scenic Boat Tours, an outfit that took tourists on relaxing cruises of Lakes Osceola, Maitland and Virginia in Winter Park, Florida, near Orlando. The tours were begun by the boat-building Meloon family, which now manufactures "Ski Nautique" water-skiing boats.

Today, Scenic Boat Tours is owned and operated by Wanda Salerno, and its pontoon boats still cruise the lakes and canals of Winter Park. Although the excursions are popular with locals as well as tourists, business has gotten a definite boost from nearby Orlando's mega-theme parks and resort destinations. People come from all over the world to see Disneyworld and Universal Studios, then catch a little real-life beauty out on the central Florida lakes.

Left, LeSene Studio, Daytona Beach, Florida, 1930s; Above, Torin Boyd, Daytona Beach, Florida

Daytona Beach in central Florida has been a popular spot for driving and dipping since the early 1900s, when turn-of-the-century tourists took their carriages for salt-air spins along 25 miles of white, hard-packed beach. By the 1920s, wealthy car enthusiasts were holding races on the sand, and in the '30s, Daytona Beach hosted a 200-mile stock car race on a course that included a 2.5-mile stretch of seashore. The last beach race for automobiles was held in 1958. The next year, the first Daytona 500 was held on a new, asphalt track constructed near the beach.

Today, cars can still cruise a 10-mile stretch of Daytona Beach, where traffic flows along at 15 miles per hour in both directions—slower during Spring Break, when tens of thousands of vacationing students crowd the waterfront.

Above, Arthur Rothstein, Grundy Center, Iowa, 1938; Right, Dana Fineman, Southfield, Michigan

Depression-era prices, like those posted in this grocer's window in Grundy Center, Iowa, above, seem a bargain today. But these were the 1930s, when nearly 20 percent of Americans were unemployed, schoolteachers earned $1,227 a year and steelworkers brought home $8 a week.

In those days, a dime could buy you a hot breakfast of eggs, potatoes and coffee. A new Pontiac coupe cost $585, and a modern six-room home with a two-car garage was just $2,800. A console radio was a splurge at almost $50, considering you could get a used 1929 Ford for just $7.50 more.

In Southfield, Michigan, today, freelance photographer Laurie Tennent, right, balks at the high prices of movies, clothing and travel, but considers fruit and vegetables a good buy. At the local Vic's Quality Fruit Market, bananas sell for 39 cents a pound—compared to seven cents in 1934. Onions have gone up 26 cents from three cents a pound during the Depression.

Left, Caufield & Shook, Mengelwood, Tennessee, 1920s; Above, Torin Boyd, Dyersburg, Tennessee

African-American "juke joints"—like this one, left, in Mengelwood, Tennessee, in 1920—were home to the blues. The word "jook" itself has African roots and was associated with partying or dancing.

In the early 1900s, African-American syncopated music and dances like the Cakewalk fascinated the American public, while appalling the more genteel members of society. Fifteen female staff members of the *Ladies' Home Journal* were fired for dancing the daring Turkey Trot on their lunch hour, and a New Jersey woman was jailed 50 days for doing this "indecent" ragtime dance. To protect its population from moral decadence, the town of Zion, Illinois, went so far as to ban the public playing of jazz in 1921.

No trace of the Mengelwood juke joint remains in the tiny Mississippi River community at Big Boy Junction. Today, the partying and dancing goes on late into a Saturday night at Cleo's, above, a small but lively club in nearby Dyersburg, Tennessee.

Above, Connecticut, 1940; Right, Jean-Pierre Laffont, Camden, Maine

Thanksgiving is probably the most venerable American holiday. First celebrated by the Plymouth colonists in 1621 to give thanks for their first harvest, a national Thanksgiving Day was proclaimed by President George Washington and made an annual holiday by Abraham Lincoln.

In 1940, at Thanksgiving time, families like the New England clan above might have fired up the Westinghouse electric range, pulled out the Hamilton Beach mixer and whipped up a traditional feast that brought back warm memories of turn-of-the-century childhoods. The menu probably included traditional treats like broiled oranges, roast turkey with celery stuffing, lima beans, and pumpkin pie washed down with lots of Chase & Sanborne coffee. After dinner? A game of Chinese checkers, or, for the young and not-too-full, some swing music on the phonograph.

For family and friends of the Rosenbergs, right, in Camden, Maine, the Thanksgiving table has many of the same staples, including roast turkey, mashed potatoes, peas and pumpkin pie.

Left, photographer and location unknown, 1930s; Above, Dana Fineman, Grosse Pointe Shores, Michigan

On Christmas morning, 1936, wide-eyed children sprinted to the tree to find out what Santa had left them. Little girls unwrapped Shirley Temple dolls and carriages, paper dolls and miniature weaving looms. Boys found "suedine" Lone Ranger vests, Buck Rogers Solar Scout badges and pocket watches and the newest "G-Men" board game.

Christmas morning for the Weiss family, above, in Grosse Pointe Shores, Michigan, is not much different today. Instead of the traditional "Santa Claus Is Coming to Town" by Eddie Cantor, it's the traditional "I'll Be Home for Christmas" by The Carpenters. But the kids get the same look in their eyes when they unwrap their loot—this year's take includes a toy electric guitar, new watch and Detroit Pistons sweatsuit for Ryan, 11, stuffed animals and a "Grabbin' Grasshoppers" game for Allison, four, and a rocking horse and plastic motorbike for "Baby Doug," two.

Boone-Holden
Austin, Tex.

Left, The Boone-Holden Photo Co., Austin, Texas, 1934
Above, Shelly Katz, Austin, Texas

In 1934, these two legendary lawmen, left, posed on the steps of the Texas State Capitol in Austin. In a picture entitled *The Reel Thing and The Real Thing*, the photographer captured Straight Shooter Tom Mix and Texas Ranger Frank H. Hamer. Mix ("The Reel Thing") made more than 400 films capturing cinematic bad guys with the help of Tony the Wonder Horse. Hamer ("The Real Thing") killed 53 real men in the line of duty, was in nearly 100 gunfights, was wounded 17 times and was left for dead four times.

Only weeks after this photograph was taken, Hamer cracked his biggest case: He tracked down and killed the notorious bank robbers Bonnie Parker, 23, and Clyde Barrow, 25. J. Edgar Hoover called Hamer "one of the greatest law officers in American history."

Today, Captain-Assistant Commander Maurice C. Cook, above, and 95 other Texas Rangers travel around the state handling special investigations and high-profile crimes like murder and armed robbery. "If the locals call us," says Cook, "we will assist."

115

Above, Arthur Rothstein, Las Vegas, Nevada, March, 1940
Right, Alice Patterson, Las Vegas, Nevada

Las Vegas was a dull desert farming and mining town until Nevada legalized gambling in 1931 and nearby Hoover Dam opened four years later. Off and on from that point forward, Las Vegas has been America's flashiest boom town—home to nine of the world's 10 largest hotels and a mecca for the over 20 million gamblers, who lay down $4 billion at the gaming tables every year.

When the three-story Apache Casino, above, opened for business in 1932, it was the pride of Glitter Gulch. The Apache featured Las Vegas' first elevator, and it was the place to see and be seen in the '30s and '40s, when the hotel drew big Hollywood names like Clark Gable and Roy Rogers.

The Hotel Flamingo, right, was built 14 years later by mobster Benjamin "Bugsy" Siegel. It opened with a bang in 1946, when headliner Jimmy Durante smashed a $1,600 piano onstage.

Norma Jean Andrew, Leonard Schutt and R.G. and Beverley Cooper, pictured outside the Flamingo, were visiting Las Vegas from Indianapolis and Surrey, British Columbia. They posed for Alice Patterson at 2:00 a.m.

Left, Weegee (Arthur Fellig), Coney Island, New York, 1940
Above, Jean-Pierre Laffont, Coney Island, New York

Brooklyn's Coney Island drew millions of sweltering, fun-seeking New Yorkers throughout the 1940s. With its hair-raising rides, sideshows and games of chance, Coney Island's amusement park and huge, white beach were New York's summer sandbox. On a hot July Sunday, as many as 1.5 million New Yorkers would crowd the waterfront.

Since the 19th century, Coney Island has alternated between periods of popularity and blight. First developed as a resort for the wealthy in the 1870s, it skidded into seedy disrepair by the early 1900s. Then, in the '20s, it was rehabilitated with a new boardwalk and connecting subway lines from Manhattan, and its popularity rose again.

By the early 1980s, however, Coney Island had once again sunk into decay. Although local treasure hunter Edward Armstrong, above, has the beach to himself on a hot October day, the pendulum may swing back again as yet another generation rediscovers its parents' playground.

119

Vernon T. Manion, Seattle, Washington, May 12, 1944

World War II was won as much by surging American industrial might as by the nation's military efforts. Above, Boeing Aircraft employees celebrate the rollout of the 5,000th B-17 bomber they built since the Japanese attack at Pearl Harbor four years earlier. The B-17 "Flying Fortress" was a state-of-the-art, four-engine bomber with a range of 3,750 miles and a top speed of 318 miles per hour.

Boeing had come a long way since the company was founded in 1916 by lumber tycoon William E. Boeing. Then it employed only 21 people, mostly carpenters and seamstresses who built and sewed the cloth skins of biplanes. By 1944, Boeing's 75,000 wartime employees were rolling out sixteen B-17s every day at a cost of $238,000 apiece.

Randy O'Brezer, Everett, Washington

Above, Boeing introduces the 747-400, the world's largest commercial jetliner. With six million parts and a wing area larger than a trio of three-bedroom homes, the giant aircraft has a top range of 8,440 miles and a cruising speed of more than 600 miles per hour. In 1991, Boeing's 141,000 employees produced five 747-400s a month, each selling for about $150 million.

Above, Acme Photos, New York, December 17, 1948
Right, Douglas Kirkland, New York, New York

Roller skates were invented by an 18th-century Belgian mechanic named Joseph Merlin. Merlin's skates could not easily turn or stop, and interest in them diminished after the inventor crashed into a mirror at a masquerade party while roller skating and playing the violin.

By the 1860s, however, improved American-made skates had captured the public interest, and the first roller rink appeared in New York City. Rollerskating hit peaks of popularity in the 1880s and early 1890s, and again in the 1930s and '40s, above, when roller-dancing was in vogue. Teenagers paired up for turns around the rink to popular tunes of the day like "Sweet Rosie O'Grady," which were played by a live organist.

Today, modern skaters can lace up their new roller-blades and glide around the rink to hip-hop music at Manhattan's Roxy Club. Although most of the week it's a dance club, the Roxy is opened for gay skating on Tuesday nights and mixed skating on Wednesdays.

Left, Red Kerce, Tallahassee, Florida, 1955; Above, Henry Groskinsky, Tallahassee, Florida

In 1955, radios were blasting Bill Haley's "Rock around the Clock," television's "As the World Turns" went on the air, and 17-year-old Ann Munroe Williamson (front, left and above) had a day in the sun as the Tallahassee May Queen.

The oldest society party in Florida, the Tallahassee May Queen Festival dated to the Civil War. May Queens were elected from the senior class of Leon High School. Williamson still remembers the excitement of the parties and photo sessions after her election and the 125 yards of white netting it took to make her antebellum-style May Queen dress.

Practically the whole town turned out for the May Queen Festival, which was held around the old May Oak in Lewis Park, and spectators craned to see the King and Queen arrive, surrounded by attendants.

In the 1960s, the plantation-era party, with its maypole dances, singers and tricycle parades, no longer seemed in step with changing times. The tradition died around the time of school integration in 1969, and the old May Oak split and fell in 1986. But for Williamson, who married the May King of 1954, the memories live on. "It was as exciting a thing as a girl could ever go through," she says today.

America: Then & Now was able to gather nine of the 16 women who appeared in the 1955 photo. One of the young women in the old picture had moved to Saudi Arabia and another to Texas, but most still lived in or near Tallahassee. Nearly all had married their high-school sweethearts and were still married to the same men almost 40 years later.

Ellsworth, Pennsylvania, 1943

In 1943, kitchen concerns were more about wartime efficiencies than decor. World War II was raging, the men were overseas, and at home, families coped with food rationing and limited supplies of butter, shortening and meat. Home-growing vegetables in a "Victory Garden" was a patriotic duty—as was saving kitchen fats in tin cans. A *Good Housekeeping* article of that year reminded its wartime readers that just one tablespoon of pan drippings helped make enough gunpowder to fire five machine-gun bullets. Lard was also recommended as a butter substitute for cooked vegetables.

Nick Kelsh, Pittsburgh, Pennsylvania

Today, working mothers like Dr. Pamela Weiss, a clinical psychologist in Pittsburgh, depend on a slew of kitchen gadgets that were unimagined in 1943. Dr. Weiss's remodeled kitchen features a trash compactor, dishwasher, microwave oven, self-lighting gas stove with electronic controls, a cordless telephone and a self-defrosting refrigerator/freezer that dispenses ice and chilled water through its door. Daughter Sophie, eight, shown here in her softball uniform, can help herself. Fats and red meats have been largely banished from the Weiss's meals for nutritional reasons, and 50 years after World War II, families once again recycle—these days, for environmental purposes.

Left, Ralph Crane, San Fernando, California, 1958
Above, Paul Chesley, San Fernando, California

In the 1950s, many Americans opted for carports and clipped lawns in suburbs like San Fernando, California. Dads went to work, moms stayed home, and babies arrived in record numbers. The boom in tots led to happy days for diaper services, which had first appeared in the 1930s.

The industry's glory days were numbered, however, the moment that Procter & Gamble introduced disposable Pampers diapers in 1961. While only 1 percent of diaper dollars went for disposables that first year, by 1990, they accounted for 85 percent of the $4.2 billion diaper market.

In 1958, Ralph Crane took this famous shot, left, illustrating the era's suburban migration and baby boom for *LIFE* magazine. *America: Then & Now*'s Paul Chesley went back 33 years later to an area that is still home to young families—now, mostly Hispanic—who came out and posed with their babies and disposables. Another difference between then and now: now, on most days, you can't see the mountains through the smog.

Above, Cornell Capa, Palisades Park, New Jersey, 1943; Right, Nick Kelsh, Woodcliff Lake, New Jersey

In the prosperous decade after World War II, America turned its attention to home, hearth and babies. The U.S. birth rate kept rising until it hit an all-time high of 4.7 million in 1957. Nuclear families headed for the newly sprouted suburbs and established the archetype of the American Dream. Above, six of the 30 million "war babies"—the first wave of the Baby Boom—compete in a Diaper Derby race in suburban Palisades Park, New Jersey.

Today, the Baby Boomers are producing a boomlet of their own, and marketers are taking note. Diaper Derbies are again showing up in malls across the country sponsored by disposable diaper manufacturer Procter & Gamble.

Less competitive parents can bring infants as young as six months to play-and-development groups like this popular Gymboree class in Woodcliff Lake, New Jersey. Gymboree provides exercise and games for babies and toddlers and gives mothers and, increasingly, fathers a chance to meet and exchange notes on teething and sleep deprivation.

Above, Oak Park, Illinois, 1959; Right, Dana Fineman, Oak Park, Illinois

In March 1959, the 13-member Brennan family posed smartly in front of their home in Oak Park, Illinois. Decked out for Chicago's annual Michigan Avenue Easter Parade, everyone wore clothes designed and sewn by their father, Thomas Brennan.

For 17 years, Mr. Brennan, the owner of a heating equipment business, tailored his family's Easter suits as a hobby. Starting just after Christmas, he selected a different theme each year. One year it was "the Dublin look," another year, "the Kennedy look." Mr. and Mrs. Brennan have passed away, but eight of the 11 Brennan children, their wives, husbands and 10 children gathered for the portrait at right on September 29, 1991. Coincidentally, photographer Dana Fineman made this portrait the day before the last Brennans left the old family home for good.

Levittown, New York, c.1951

As World War II ended, millions of victorious young war veterans had new wives, new babies and no affordable housing. Developer William Levitt met this need with an audacious and typically American scheme. If cars, tanks and airplanes could be mass-produced, why not houses?

From 1947 to 1951, Levitt and Sons turned 1,200 acres of Long Island potato fields into a planned community complete with schools, shopping centers and playgrounds. Over 17,000 pre-fab, four-room houses were built at the rate of 12 houses per day.

The $8,000 Levitt house included a TV, washing machine and barbecue. Levittown homes were sold to white veterans only, and for as little as $20 down.

Jean-Pierre Laffont, Levittown, New York

Over the past 45 years, most of the cookie-cutter Levitt houses have been remodeled as Swiss chalets, American colonials or Tudor manors. Trees, shrubs and lawns cover the old potato fields, and grandchildren of the young GIs who bought the original Levittown houses play in the yards. Remodeled or expanded homes now sell for $160,000 or more, and few of the original ranch and Cape Cod models, with their white metal kitchen cabinets and distinctive Levittown door knockers, remain. Ironically, these are now considered historic landmarks—the last of the original tract houses.

Above, H. Armstrong Roberts II, New York, New York, c.1947
Right, Douglas Kirkland, New York, New York

La Guardia Airport opened to commercial traffic on December 2, 1939, just in time for the New York World's Fair. Named after Fiorello La Guardia, the popular New York mayor of that time, its bayside site was originally the home of the Gala Amusement Park.

When La Guardia first opened, families drove over on Sunday afternoons just to watch the planes take off and land. Airport passengers were mostly wealthy adventurers travelling to Europe on trans-Atlantic "clipper" aircraft—sea planes that could make ocean landings if necessary.

Over the years, as air travel became more accessible to the middle class, traffic boomed at La Guardia. In 1949, when the picture above was probably taken, the airport processed over three million passengers and nearly 160,000 takeoffs and landings. Now, annual passenger traffic has increased nearly 10-fold, and few reminders are left of the time when every airplane trip was a glamorous adventure.

Left, North Carolina, 1932; Above, Henry Groskinsky, Durham, North Carolina

Radio took to the air in 1920, and within two years Americans were spending $60 million on radios ranging from do-it-yourself crystal sets to Crosley table-top models and inlaid consoles. From remote Texas farmhouses to Newport mansions, Americans tuned in to scratchy broadcasts of popular songs like "Yes, We Have No Bananas" and news bulletins from Floyd Gibbons. Even during the darkest years of the Depression, Americans kept buying and listening to radios—four million sets were sold from 1930 to 1932. Personalities like Jack Benny and Eddie Cantor and shows like "The Shadow" and "Fibber McGee and Molly" entertained listeners and turned their minds from their troubles.

News, too, was more dramatic on the radio. For the first time, on-air correspondents could report news on the spot, as it happened.

In the 1930s, live coverage involved strapping 30 pounds of remote relay equipment to the backs of a reporter, an engineer and a third volunteer. This three-man team, left, was from WPTF in Raleigh, North Carolina. Owned by the Durham Insurance Company, WPTF stood for "We Protect the Family." Today, above, radio reporters like WPTF's Mike Blackman can use a cellular phone or a briefcase-size portable transmitter that weighs less than six pounds. Blackman's most memorable live broadcast: "The crash of a plane carrying the Army's entire Golden Knight Parachute team in a town ironically named Silk Hope, North Carolina."

Left, General Electric and U.S. Army Ordnance, Cape Canaveral, Florida, 1950
Above, Roger Scruggs, Cape Canaveral, Florida

On July 24, 1950, photographers chronicled the launch of Bumper 8, the first rocket to take off from the new American facility at Cape Canaveral, Florida. Although the U.S. has two other launch sites in California and Virginia, Cape Canaveral and its Kennedy Space Center have been the focal point of the American space effort for the past four decades.

The space race began on October 5, 1957 when the Soviets put Sputnik 1—a two-foot diameter sphere—into orbit. Less than a month later came Sputnik 2—a 1,000-pound satellite carrying a live dog. The first U.S. attempt to put a six-inch satellite into orbit blew up on the launch pad. In the context of the Cold War, these early Soviet successes—and the spectacular American failure—took on cosmic significance. Soviet rockets could deliver satellites into orbit (and atomic weapons to America); ours blew up on the pad. Politicians reacted, and from that point forward, Saturn rockets and "right stuff" astronauts became a national passion.

Today, reusable space shuttles ferry satellites in and out of earth orbit, and space shots seem nearly commonplace. Only when the 25th shuttle flight exploded on January 28, 1986, killing all aboard, was the country reminded that risk and heroism were still part of the mission.

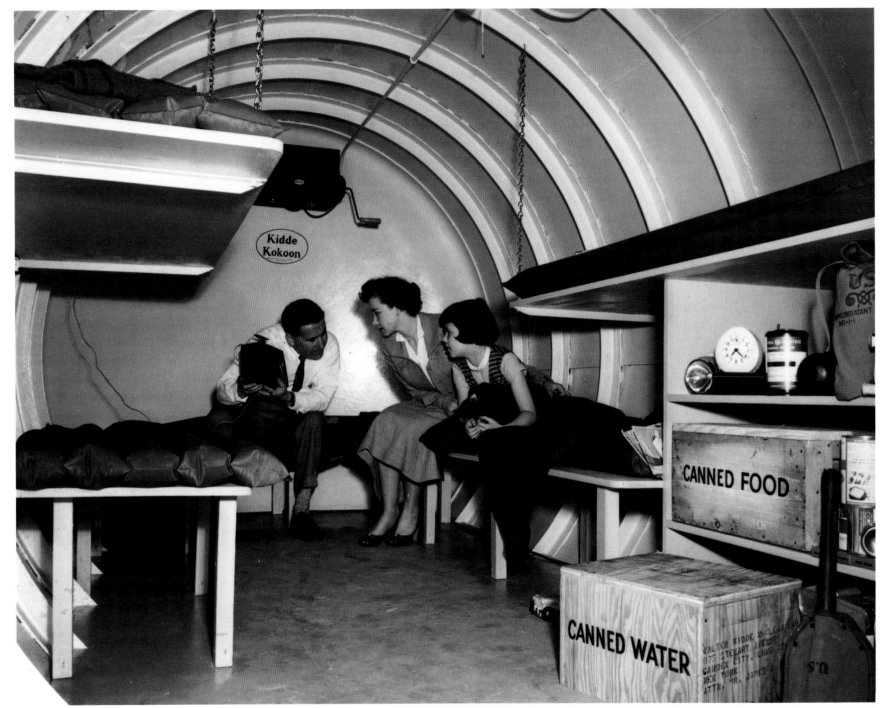

Garden City, New York, c.1955

After the widely publicized American hydrogen bomb tests at Bikini atoll in 1954 and the establishment of the communist Warsaw Pact in 1955, the Cold War between the U.S. and the U.S.S.R. seemed to be heating up. Schools across America held "duck and cover" drills—apparently thinking that school desks could provide protection from Soviet hydrogen bombs—and some families began to build well-stocked basement bomb shelters.

This widespread fear of atomic attack created opportunities for savvy marketers. Walter Kidde Nuclear Laboratories of Garden City, N.Y., offered the comforts of their Kidde Kokoon, guaranteed to keep a family safe three feet underground during a nuclear attack.

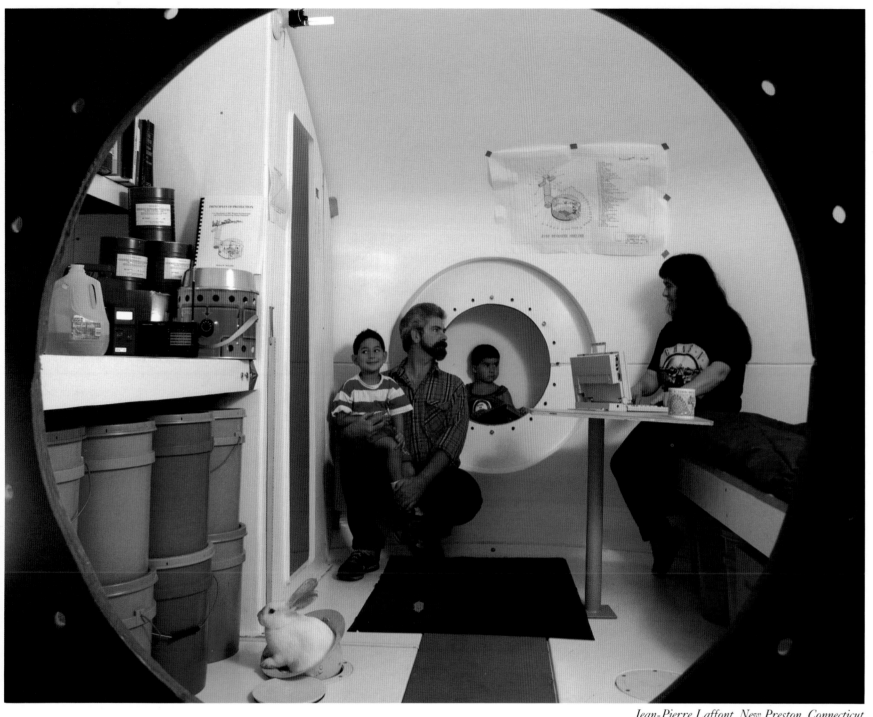

Jean-Pierre Laffont, New Preston, Connecticut

Today, families that want protection from nuclear, biological and chemical attack, hurricanes and earthquakes can climb into the newest generation ES-10 Disaster Shelter, developed by Subtech of Northwood, New Hampshire. Buried 15½ feet below the ground, the shelter comes equipped with a command station, decontamination area and optional nuclear, biological and chemical warfare filters. The ES-10 can protect 10 people for 30 days after a major disaster—man-made or natural—and comes with a 30-year warranty. Walton McCarthy, Subtech's president says, "Among our best customers are congressmen, government analysts and the IRS, which has contingency plans to collect taxes after an atomic attack."

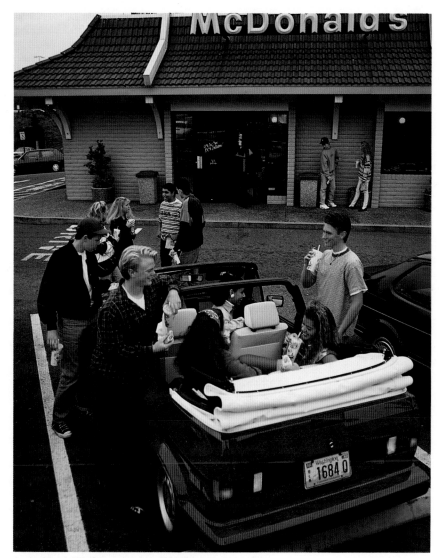

Left, Hank Walker, suburban Washington, DC, 1956
Above, Ed Lowe, Seattle, Washington

First there was the hamburger, then the car (or was it the other way around?). Anyway, when the two concepts collided in the 1940s, the drive-in diner was born. The result was irresistible to teenagers. Post-war, southern high-schoolers would "go frogging" (cruising) and scarf hamburgers after a ball game. In the '50s, "carhops"—sometimes on roller skates— would deliver fresh orders of burgers, fries, fried chicken and shakes.

Today, the great mass of burger gulping kids patronize huge chains like McDonald's. The first of what is now more than 12,000 McDonald's opened in 1955, cutting out frills like carhops and long menus. But with 15-cent burgers and 25-cent shakes, the concept caught on. Over 35 years later, teens from Seattle's Ingram and Nathan Hale High still drive over to the local McDonald's, above, which serves up 1,500 burgers and 355 pounds of fries a day. You can still order from your car, of course, but nowadays it's through an intercom.

Left, Francis Miller, c.1955; Above, Shelly Katz, Dallas, Texas

In December 1945, 81 percent of Gallup Poll respondents said they had never seen TV. Six years later, 10 million American families owned sets.

Americans demonstrated a huge appetite for shows like *I Love Lucy, The Lone Ranger* and *Kukla, Fran and Ollie*, and kids, especially, were turned on by the tube. In 1950, children, on average, were watching 27 hours of television a week (slightly more than now), and Boston University President Daniel Marsh lamented that "we are destined to have a nation of morons."

In 1955, left, young baby boomers were entertained by *Davy Crockett, Gunsmoke* and *Captain Kangaroo*. (That's Fess Parker as Davy Crockett on the screen.) Today, these four-year-old Teenage Mutant Ninja Turtle fans, above, can choose from four broadcast networks, two dozen cable channels, videotaped movies, interactive video games and compact discs that project random access video encyclopedias and books onto their screens.

Stern Bramson, Louisville, Kentucky, late 1950s

In 1954, Elvis Aaron Presley was a 19-year-old truck driver earning $35 a week in Memphis. Two years later, under the management of "Colonel" Tom Parker, Elvis was the king of rock 'n' roll and international hero to a generation of young people. Elvis's velvet voice, sneering, sexy attitude and shocking hip gyrations sold 13.5 million singles and nearly three million albums in 1956 alone, but that was only part of the Presley bonanza. The same year, fans shelled out $20 million at stores across the country—like this Kitty Kelly shoe store in Louisville, Kentucky—for "official" Elvis merchandise, ranging from jewelry, statuettes and dolls to bubblegum cards, rings, perfume and lipstick in shades of Tutti Frutti Red and Hound Dog Orange.

Torin Boyd, Memphis, Tennessee

More than a decade after Presley's death, Elvis merchandise is selling more than ever, and his former Memphis home, Graceland, has become a sort of secular shrine for millions of die-hard fans. Graceland-bound fans looking for more relics of "The King" can browse in stores like this Memphis newsstand for Presley mugs, license plates, statuette-decanters with screw-on Elvis heads, commemorative plates and "Love Me Tender" milk bath and shampoo.

Henry Grossman, 1963

In 1963, teenage girls rolled their hair in jumbo, baby pink curlers while listening to stacks of 45s on portable hi-fis. The Platters, Dion and Paul and Paula recorded heartthrob hits that year, while Chubby Checker had the nation twisting the night away. Most of the music of the time was pretty light and apolitical, but the times, they were a-changin'. Bob Dylan and Peter, Paul and Mary were at the vanguard of American folk, and a recently formed English group, The Beatles, had just recorded the hit song "Love Me Do."

Jay O'Neil, Novato, California

Today, teenagers like these in Novato, California, are more likely to pop in a cassette tape or compact disc than play an old-fashioned vinyl record. They wear headphones, not curlers, and the music of the moment is rap and hip-hop. Favorite bands on the day this picture was taken included BBD, Boys to Men, Yo Yo, Hi Five and Public Enemy.

Washington Post, *1964*

On "B-Day," February 7, 1964, Beatlemania swept America. Screaming, fainting, crying, frenzied fans mobbed New York's Kennedy Airport to catch a glimpse of four shaggy-headed lads who had already become a teenage obsession in Britain. John Lennon, 23, Paul McCartney, 21, George Harrison, 21, and Ringo Starr, 23, had already sold six million records. They scored the highest TV rating in U.S. history when they appeared on the *Ed Sullivan* show later that week. The Beatles ended their 33-day U.S. tour with a gross of $2.1 million. America "was fantastic," said Ringo. "They all seem out of their minds."

Lynn Goldsmith, on tour with New Kids on the Block

Today (and for a while after this book is printed), thousands of mousse-haired teenagers hysterically mob concerts of New Kids on the Block, a band that has sold more than 14 million albums since 1988. Hailing from Boston, the band's wholesome-looking quartet blend Motown and Main Street in a formula that has made them one of the most financially successful groups in pop music—ever. The band rakes in $125,000 a night at sold-out concerts across the country and earns millions more in lucrative licensing agreements. Los Angeles radio programmer Steve Rivers, for one, would not compare the New Kids to the Beatles musically. "But for those who remember the early stages of Beatlemania," he says, "the enthusiasm is similar."

Above, New York Daily Mirror, *November 14, 1959*
Right, Douglas Kirkland, New York, New York

Rebels against the prim, middle-class morality and materialism of the post-war years, Beats, above, flocked to the cafes and coffeehouses of San Francisco's North Beach and New York's Greenwich Village. Clad in leather jackets and tight jeans, they hung out in smokey clubs like The Cock 'n Bull, Caffe Cino and the Gaslight, listening to folk and jazz, sipping cappuccinos in mugs and nodding to the Beat verse of poets like Allen Ginsberg and Lawrence Ferlinghetti.

Forty years later, at CBGB's, a rock club in Manhattan's Bowery area, musicians like Brian Childers, Alice Cohen and Paul Bearer, right, declare their own rebellion with dreadlocks, pierced noses and tattoos. Bands appearing at CBGB's include avant-garde rockers like Crawl Pappy and Die Monster Die. Times change, the names change, but the idea is still the same—create a counter-culture, shock society, shake up the world a bit.

Left, Tupperware, 1960; Above, Alice Patterson, Roseville, California

Every 2.7 seconds, from Munich to Miami Beach, there is a Tupperware party somewhere in the world. First marketed in 1945 by inventor Earl Tupper, the polyethylene Tupperware containers helped launch the plastics craze of the early 1950s. Wonderlier bowl sets, Spaghetti Dispensers, Pick-a-Deli lunch-meat containers and some 200 other products have made their way into 90 percent of American kitchens and more than 40 countries around the world. Fifteen of the earliest Tupperware designs are housed in the permanent design collection of New York's Museum of Modern Art.

Throughout the 1950s, '60s and '70s, the products were sold mostly by homemakers who made extra income hosting two-hour daytime Tupperware Home Parties for their friends. As in the 1960 get-together, left, this sales approach combined party games and contests with product demonstrations.

Today, independent Tupperware manager Stephanie Garber in Roseville, California, above, hosts shorter parties in the evening to meet the schedules of busy, two-income families. Door prizes and "get-to-know-you" games like recipe swapping are still part of the Tupperware approach, but microwave cooking classes, food freezing classes, "Rush Hour Parties" and even environmental courses now account for a growing portion of sales. Tupperware is the fad that never died. New products include microwave cooking containers, the Tortilla Keeper, marketed in Mexico, and the Kimono Keeper, sold only in Japan.

Left, H. Armstrong Roberts II, early 1960s
Above, Paul Chesley, Los Angeles, California

In the 1920s, swimming pools were splashy playthings for the rich. But by the 1950s, inexpensive construction techniques had brought pool prices within the range of middle-class homeowners. Industry promoters called backyard pools "a logical extension of the family television room," and cultural observers considered them a hallmark of the newly affluent America. The number of residential pools swelled from 30,000 in 1948 to 300,000 in 1963, left, and to a million in the early '70s.

Today, 3.4 million American families have swimming pools in their backyards, from shallow lap pools to extravagant, "natural" models featuring waterfalls and artificial rock. Peter and Donna Lance, above, and their children, Christopher, four, and Mallory, two, love to splash in their 1950s, scallop-shaped pool in Los Angeles, which they've updated with a robotic pool sweep and a solar-powered cover.

159

Trans World Airlines, St. Louis, Missouri, March 22, 1967

Founded by the French in 1764, St. Louis was the hub of America's westward expansion in the early 19th-century. This was after Thomas Jefferson nearly doubled the land area of the United States with his $15 million Louisiana Purchase in 1803. To commemorate the westward migration, the Gateway Arch National Monument was erected on the Mississippi riverfront in 1965. The stainless-steel-clad, 630-foot Gateway Arch was designed by the renowned Finnish architect Eero Saarinen, who won the commission in a design contest. It was photographed, above, in 1967, from the window of the last TWA Constellation on that airline's last propeller-driven passenger flight.

Dana Fineman, St. Louis, Missouri

More than 2.5 million tourists a year visit the Gateway Arch today and ride the trams inside its legs to the observation platform above the Mississippi. At the top of the arch, in the middle of America, the words of the French politician and writer Alexis de Tocqueville seem especially farsighted. He wrote of America, "Millions of men are marching at once toward the same horizon; their language, their religion, their manners differ; their object is the same. Fortune has been promised to them somewhere in the West, and to the West they go to find it…"

COLORADO
Denver
4
29
Leadville
60
61
Pueblo
28

WYOMING
Cheyenne
19
76
77
Newcastle
18

NEBRASKA
Cherry County
26
Comstock
13
East Custer County
12
Omaha
3
Oshkosh
27

SOUTH DA
Lantry
82
83
Pine Ridge
10
11
Rapid City
88
89
90
91

WASHINGTON
Colville
53
Eastern Washington
52
Everett
121
Orting
17
Port Blakely
38
Seattle
39
120
145
Western Washington
16

CALIFORNIA
Hollywood
84
85
86
87
Los Angeles
45
159
Merced
75
Novato
151
Pasadena
41
Roseville
157
San Fernando
128
129
San Francisco
74
100
101
Yosemite Valley
54
55

NEVADA
Las Vegas
116
117

TEXAS
Austin
114
115
Dallas
93
147
Fort Bliss
9
Marfa
92

UNKNOWN LOCATIONS
8, 40, 112, 146, 150, 152, 153, 156, 158

MINNESOTA
Minneapolis
9

ILLINOIS
Chicago
98
99
Oak Park
132
133

MISSOURI
St. Louis
68
160
161

IOWA
Grundy Center
106

INDIANA
Speedway
56
57

MICHIGAN
Dearborn
71
Detroit
170
Grosse Pointe Shores
113
Highland Park
70
Southfield
107
Troy
171

PENNSYLVANIA
46
Ellsworth
126
Kennett Square
47
Philadelphia
69
Pittsburgh
48
49
50
51
127
Pottstown
62
63
Red ington
72
Scranton
73
South Pittston
66
67

MASSACHUSETTS
Boston
24
25
58

MAINE
Camden
111
Pumpkin Island
38
39

CONNECTICUT
110
New Haven
20
21
New Preston
143

NEW YORK
Arkville
33
Catskills
32
Cooperstown
5
Coney Island
118
119
Garden City
142
Levittown
134
135
New York City
44
94
95
96
97
122
123
136
137
154
155
Sayeville
171

NEW JERSEY
Palisades Park
130
Woodcliff Lake
131

WASHINGTON, DC
6
7

MARYLAND
Annapolis
22
23

64
65
78
79
144

WEST VIRGINIA
Morgantown
34
35

NORTH CAROLINA
138
Durham
139

KENTUCKY
Louisville
148

TENNESSEE
Chatanooga
30
31
Dyersburg
109
Memphis
80
81
149
Mengelwood
108

FLORIDA
Cape Canaveral
140
141
Daytona Beach
104
105
Everglades
14
Miami
15
Tallahassee
124
125
Winter Park
102
103

ALABAMA
Tuskegee
42
43

163

Acknowledgements

Picture Sources

American Telephone & Telegraph Company, p. 40

The Bettmann Archive, including the UPI
and New York Daily Mirror collections, pp. 78, 110, 112, 122, 132, 134, 154

Bison Archives, pp. 84, 86

The Boeing Company, p. 120

Boston Public Library, pp. 3, 58

Caterpillar Tractor Company, p. 52

Colorado State Historical Society, p. 60

Culver Pictures, p. 118

Denver Public Library, Western History Collection, p. 4

The District of Columbia Public Library, Washington Post Collection, p.152

Florida State Archives, pp. 14, 104, 124

Ford Motor Company, p. 70

Frinzi Studios, p. 21

General Electric Company/U.S. Army Ordnance, p. 140

Golden Gate Bridge, Highway and Transportation District, p. 100

H. Armstrong Roberts, pp. 136, 158

Hagley Museum and Library, pp. 88, 126

Indianapolis Motor Speedway Corporation, p. 56

The International Museum of Photography at George Eastman House, pp. 8, 46, 66

LGI Photo Agency, p. 153

Kmart Corporation Archives, pp. 169, 170, 171

Library of Congress, Prints and Photographs Division,
pp. 1, 10, 24, 28, 30, 32, 36, 42, 54, 62, 68, 70, 74, 80, 96, 106, 116, 142

Life Picture Service (all from Life Magazine © Time Warner, Inc.),
pp . 128, 130, 144, 146, 150

The National Archives, p. 98

National Geographic Society, courtesy of U.S. Supreme Court Historical Society, p. 65

Nebraska State Archives, (Solomon D. Butcher Collection), pp. 12, 26

New York Public Library, p. 44

New York State Historical Association, Cooperstown, p. 5

Orange County Historical Society, Florida, p. 102

Pennsylvania Historical and Museum Commission, p. 48

Roger Scruggs Films, p. 140

San Francisco Maritime Museum, p. 38

Staten Island Historical Society, p. 22

Supreme Court of the United States, p. 64

Timber Lake and Area Historical Society, South Dakota, p. 82

Trans World Airlines, p. 160

Tupperware Home Parties, p. 156

University of Louisville, Photographic Archives, pp. 108, 148

University of North Carolina at Chapel Hill, North Carolina Collection, p. 138

University of Texas at Austin, Barker Texas History Center, p. 114

The University of Texas at Austin,
Harry Ransom Humanities Research Center, Gernsheim Collection, p. 92

The Office of the Architect of the U.S. Capitol, p. 6

The Estate of James Van Der Zee, p. 94

West Virginia University Library, West Virginia and Regional History Collection, p. 34

Whatcom Museum of History and Art (Darius Kinsey Collection), pp. 16, 166

Wyoming State Archives, Museums and Historical Department, pp. 18, 76

Yale University Library, p. 20

Organizations

Literally hundreds of organizations and individuals cooperated in the making of this book. They have our sincere gratitude.

Abrams & Associates
American Airlines
American Photo Archive
American Heritage Library
American Swedish Institute
Arch
Aspen Graphics
Aspen Historical Society
Austin Public Library, Austin History Center
The Bank of America, Mill Valley, California
Barker History Center
Beacon Historical Society
Beltrami County Historical Society
The Bettmann Archive
Big Bend Sentinel
The Boeing Company
Boston Public Library
Tom Bradley International Airport
Broken Bow Historical Society
Brown Brothers
The Burns Archive
BWC Photolabs
Castle Air Force Base
Carnegie County Historical Society
Carpenter Center of Photography Archive
Center for Creative Photography
Champion Paper Corporation
Chattanooga Regional History Museum
Chesapeake Bay Maritime Museum
Chevy Chase Historical Society
The Chrysler Building
Colorado Springs Gazette
Colorado State Historical Society
Consolidated Coal
Culver Pictures
Curt Teich Postcard Archives/
Lake County Museum
Dallas Historical Society
Denver Public Library,
Western History Collection
Vin DiBono Productions
The District of Columbia Public
Library, Washington Post Collection
Douglas County Museum of History
Drug Enforcement Agency
Florida State Archives
Ford Motor Company
Fresno City & County Historical Society
Frinzi Studios
Gale Memorial Library
Gallatin County Historical Society
Galveston Park Board of Trustees
George Eastman House
Gold's Gym, Galveston, Texas
Golden Gate Bridge Highway &
Transportation District
Grand County Historical Association
Gymboree
H. Armstrong Roberts
Hagley Museum and Library
Harris County Heritage Society

Harry Ransom Humanities Research Center,
The University of Texas at Austin
Hawaiian Historical Society
Henry Ford Museum & Greenfield Village
Hidalgo County Historical Museum
Historical Society of Washington, DC
ICS
Immigrant City Archives
Indian Hill Historical Society
Indianapolis Motor Speedway Corporation
The International Museum of Photography
at George Eastman House
Ivey Seright International
Johns Hopkins University
Kennedy Space Center
KGBC Galveston
Koochiching County Historical Society
LGI
Library of Congress, Prints and Photographs
Division
Life Picture Service
Louisiana State University/Shreveport
Archives
Maine State Archives
Matteson Historical Society
Mill Valley Services
Museum of New Mexico
NASA, Johnson Space Center
National Anthropological Archives
The National Archives
National Geographic Society
National Museum of Rollerskating
The National Organization of Women
The National Park Service, Mt. Rushmore
Nebraska State Archives
New York Public Library
New York State Historical Association,
Cooperstown
Nez Perce County Historical Society
Orange County Historical Society (Florida)
Pacific Bell
Park Forest Historical Society
Pasadena Public Library
Peale Museum, Baltimore City Life Museum
Pennsylvania Historical and
Museum Commission
Piggly Wiggly
Pinnacle Publishing Services
The Pottstown Police Force
Putnam County Archives and
History Commission
Rath Community Museum,
Pittsburgh, Pennsylvania
Railway & Locomotive
Historical Society, Inc.
Rhode Island Museum of Art
Roger Scruggs Films
San Francisco Maritime Museum
Shrimp Boat Restaurant
Silviane Pagent Productions
Smith Library of Regional History
Southbury Historical Society, Inc.
Staten Island Historical Society
Sullivan County Chamber of Commerce
Supreme Court Historical Society

Supreme Court of the United States
Sygma
Talafierro County Historical Society
Timber Lake and Area Historical Society, South Dakota
The Carbon Alternative
The San Francisco Public Library
Tupperware Home Parties
Tuskegee University
The Union Pacific Railroad
Uniphoto
The Office of the Architect of the United States Capitol
United States Army, 3rd Cavalry Regiment
The United States Capitol Police
University of Louisville, Photographic Archives and Ekstrom Library
United States Naval Academy
University of North Carolina at Chapel Hill, North Carolina Collection
University of Texas at Austin, Barker Texas History Center
US Geologic Survey Library
The Estate of James Van Der Zee
Virginia Commonwealth University
Washington State Historical Society
Wells Fargo Bank, Mill Valley Branch
Western Hardware Company, Museum & Emporium
West Virginia University Library, West Virginia and Regional History Collection
Whatcom Museum of History and Art
White Pillars Museum
Wide World Photos
The Women's Civic League of Cheyenne, Wyoming
Workman & Temple Family Homestead Museum
Wyoming State Archives, Museum and Historical Department
Yale Sports Information
Yale University Library

Advisors, Consultants and Friends

Joseph Abrams
Heather Akawie
Leslie S. Alberti
Irenio Alejo
Peter Allen
Billy Amberg
Mike Ames
Enriquez Analia
James C. Anderson
Lois Anderton
Norma Jean Andrew
Tom & Mary Angelo
Himawana Apiwibowo
Ken Ariolo, Capt., USAF
Edward Armstrong
Bob Arnott
Larry M. Asbell
Herb and Dorothy Ascherman
Paul Ash
Rebecca Atkinson
Maria Victoria Auge
Joey Baldino
Anna Maria Bambara
Michael Banks
Robert Banks
Judith Banning
Adelaide Barbey
Bill Barlow
Caroline Barnes
Jenny Barry
W. Henry Bass

Nancy Bath
Paul Bearer
Guillermo Beauchamp
Barbara Belcher Rayborn
Andy & Sam Belt
Eliane Benisti
Kevin Bentley
Mark Berger
Rod Bergiel
Steve Berl
Luigi Bernabo
Pam Beyers
Bipin, Bharti, Prashant & Samit Bhayani
Carole Bidnick
David Biehn
William Bigelow
Dr. Herman P. and Elaine Binger
Adeline LaToya Rose Black Elk
Charlotte Black Elk
Henry Louis Black Elk
Leonard Benjamin Black Elk
Mickeylea B. Black Elk
Tatoye Najinwin Emma Black Elk
Mikki Black Elk & Family
Mike Blackman
Alice J. Blackwell
Jason Blantz
Desa Rae Blevins
Anita Bloch
Sandra J. Boen
Un Jong Bong
Rebecca Booth
Jim Bowles, Capt. USAF
John Boyle
Reginald Brack, Jr.
Julie Bradrick
Elizabeth Bradshaw
Gulla Britt Brann
Herman Brann
Oscar Brann
Patrick L. Braswell
Eric Breitbard
Brian C. Brennan
Claudia D. Brennan
Devon Brennan
Eamon Brennan
Jane S. Brennan
Joan Brennan
Kieran C. Brennan
Michael Brennan
Patrick T. Brennan
Seamus P. Brennan
Sean D. Brennan
Seamus P. Brennan, Jr.
Barbara & Stuart Brenner
Angela M. Brewer
Jack Brewer
Karl A. Bridge
Marcia Brogan
Esther Bromberg
John Bromley
Carole E. Brotherton
Jim Brown
Julie Brumleve
Tali Buchman
Amy Buckner
Valgene A. Buckner
Scott Budny
Jennifer Buffaloe
Laura, Leah & Michael Buono
Paul Burgin
Dr. Stanley Burns
Heather Burns
Allison Busch
Renee J. Buston
Robert W. Buston
Pat Butera

Aine M. Byans
Pam Byers
Samantha Calderon
Carla Callis
Robert Cameron
Woodfin Camp
David Candy
David M. Caplan
Toni Cardoza
Clayton Carlson
Glenn Carlson, Capt. USAF
Jorge Casali
Monica Casali
Norma Casali
Shannan Casey
Carmen Castro
Max T. Catt
Robert Cave-Rogers
Mike Cerre
Ani Chamichian
Suzan Chapman
Howard Chapnick
James Cheevers
Anthony Chemero
Padmini Chetty
Brian Childers
Donald L. Childress
John A. Chinni
Linda Christenson
Arta Christiansen
Dale & June Christiansen
Shirley Christine
Albert Chu
Donna Chung
John Cimo
Alexander & Michael Claes
Helen Clark
Tracy Allen Clark
Lisabeth Coakley
William Coblentz
Ken Coburn
Alice Cohen
Daniel Cohen
Debra Cohen
Kara Cohen
Norman & Hannah Cohen
Steve, Ellen, Aliza & Sara Cohen
William G. K. Cohen
Gail A. Cole
Chuck, Paula, Sarah & Julia Collins
Ray & Meredith Collins
Kathleen Condon
Dorian Conley
Cassy Conroy
Priscilla Contreras
Caroline Conway
Bill Cook
Colin Cook
Elaine Cook
Maurice Cook
Beverley B. Cooper
Guy Cooper
R.G. Cooper
Marjorie Corn
Thomas J. Coscarelli
Joanna Cotler
Jerry Cotten
Deborah Sue Cox
Joseph M. Cox
Eric Cozens
George Craig
Dexter Curtis
Celeste G. Daniels
Bob David
Malka David
Robert E. David
Tony David
Dick Davidson

Paula Davis
Phil & Beverly Davis
Agnes de Gouvion Saint Cyr
Doug De Laune
Emily De Laune
Laurie De Laune
Shalina De Laune
João De Macedo
Sophie de Sivry
Cynthia Dearwater
Brian Deasy
Kathy Deatherage
Vera Deatherage
Cliff Deeds
Carlotta DeFillio
Ray DeMoulin
Eartha Dengler
Sandie Dent
John DePetrillo
Marina Devoulin
Vin Di Bona
Mark Dibrelli, Capt., USAF
Craig Dickgieser
Chickie Diogardi
Sean Dodge
Sven Dolling
Sheila Donnelly
Louis Douget
Curtis and Dorothy Dowse
Eleanor Dowse
Philip Dowse
Ron Dowse
Arnold Drapkin
Ronald Drews
Beth Dungan
Barbara Dunn
Oscar Dystel
Jim Dziura
Lois Eagleton
Cheryl Eastman
David Eastman
Carol Eberdardt
Dr & Mrs. Richard Eisenberg
Roy Eisenhardt
Sandra Eisert
Ralph Elder
Valerie E. Elliott
Kathryn Ellison
Melody Ennis
Tona Enriquez
Jeffrey & Susan Epstein
Laurel Epstein
Louis & Esther Epstein
Stanley & Sylvia Epstein
Jennifer Erwitt
Becky W. Evans
Heather Evans
Lynn Falls
David & Eleanor Fax
Maureen Fay
Philip, Lisa & Hope Feldman
Mark S. Fetterman
Joanne Finkelstein
Mary Fiori
Bill Fitzgerald
James Flanagan
Paul Fleming
Linda Fontana
Sally B. Foot
Carole Ford
Angelique Foreman
James Fox
Adam Frank
Jack and Mia Freilich
Miriam Friars
Anthony Frias
Rolfe Fricke
Briggs Gamblin

Craig Garcia
Carolyn L. Garner
Douglas Tyroner Garner
Akira Gatsuura
Ali Ghalebi
Michael Glasco
Lara Goldbeck
Raymond and Betty Jean Goldblum
Charlotte & Ed Gordon
Tinka Gordon
Linden Goss
John Gotleib
Marty & Beryl Graboff
Tom Grady
Frances P. Graham
Karen, Bradley, Samantha & Aaron Graham
Christopher Grant
Pat & Mary Grant
William & Mary Agnes Grant
Jason R. Gray
Vincent Gray
Jeff B. Gray & Friends
Jake Greenmeyer
Janet Greenmeyer
Victor Greto
Jennifer Groom
Robert Groves
Jim Guidry
Reginald K. Guidry
Stephanie Gunn
Jason Hackett
David, Susan, Emily & Casey Hagerman
Carl Haight-Boy
Katherine Hamilton-Smith
Lisa Hancock
Nicole Harper
Utana R. Harrington
Nick Harris
Michael W. Harrison
Ed Hart
Tim Harvey
Douglas Hase
Leigh Hatayma
Helen Hayes
Patricia Hayes
Jean Hazelwood
Maureen Healy
Francois Hebel
William Heimdahl
Sally Hekkers
Dr. Fred Henderson
Joseph Henderson
Lyn Henley
Otilia & Vanessa Hernandez
Caroline Herter
Derek Hess
Bill & Terri Higgins
Nancy Higgins
Steve Hilderman
Catherine M. Hines
Laura Hines
Steve Hirsen
Rebecca Hirsh
Fred Hoch
Marc, Nadine & Noah Hoffman
Tom Hoffman
Chuck Holland
David Holland
Gary Holmberg
Kimio Honda
Nick & Nancy Hoppe
Dan Horan
Richard Horowitz
Brian Horrigan
Robert Horton
Ruth Howe

Kent Scott
Trey Scott
William Scoville
Robin Seaman
Dennis Seibel
Rob & Annette Shapiro
Pat Sheppard
Steve, Dana, Caty & Alex Sherman
Sykvia J. Sherman
Keva Sieber
Damon Silverman
Erin Simmons
Ethan Simon
Michael Singer
Nancy P. Sinsel
Margaret & Bill Sircher
Meghan, Molly & Sean Sircher
Rev. Francis Skelly
Silvia Sleight
Catherine W. Smith
Ronald Lee Smith
Eva Solovay
Barbara Sorenson
June M. Staackman
Mistie Standley
Stanton W. Starr
Christine M. Stearns
Dieter Steiner
Donna Stephens-Cianni
Michele Stephenson
Jay Stevens
Vic Stevens
Christopher Stewart
Ed Stewart
James & Virginia Stewart
Timothy Stewart
Neil Stillmock
Rachel Stires
John Clay Stites
Tim Stokes
Neil G. Stone
Laureena Stoutenburg
Lew Stowbunenko
Teresa M. Straub
Laura Street
Blanche Streeter
Charles Styles
Nina Svoboda
Kathy Swan
Julie L. Swanson
Carol Sykes
Stewart Tabakin
Jeffrey M. Tait
Yukio Takeshige
Jon R. Tandler
Jody Tang
Charles Taylor
Graham & Dr. Nancy Taylor
Laurie Tennent
Sarah Tennent
Dee Terry
Chris Tetens
Todd Thicke
Melissa Thomas
Norman and Lydia Thompson
Jordan Thorn
Kris Tomanek
Fay Torresyap
Meredith Tromble
Pete Turner
John Ugoretz
Kevin T. Ulbert
Kim Ulbert
Kathleen T. Ulbert, Jr.
Michael E. Ulbert, Jr.
Kathleen T. Ulbert, Sr.
Michael E. Ulbert, Sr.
Steven Ulrich

Ricardo N. Valadez
Denise Van Buren
Mrs. Donna Van Der Zee
Caroline van Gelderen
Julia Van Haaften
Katrina Van Houten
Julie Vardiman
Melanie Varin
Cynthia Vasquez
Frances Vasquez
Maria Vasquez
Reina Vasquez
Travelyn Vasquez
Vianey Vasquez
Lisa Velazquez
Susan Vermazen
Martha Vestecka-Mille
Rudy Vetter
Chris Villiers
Henry Von Spreckesen
Karen Graham Wade
Judy Waggoner
Stewart Wahl
Gilbert J. Wahl, Jr.
Barbara Walanin
Jordan, Les & Sandra Waldman
Hal Walker
Nancy Walsh
Marguerite Wamsley
Marc Wanamaker
Ben & LiLi Wang
Stephanie Ward
Kathy Warnock
Christine V. Warren
Wellington Webb
Jane D. Webster
Deborah Weinberg
Glenn Weinberg
Laura Weinberg
Marc Weinberg
Shelley Weinberg
David Weintraub
Carl & Conrad Weisensee
Allison Weiss
Leslie Rauen Weiss
Pamela Weiss
Ryan Weiss
Douglas Weiss, Jr.
Douglas Arthur Weiss, Sr.
Michael Wellman
Dan Wenk
Heidi Werbel
Len Wesson
Caitlin West
Eric Weyenberg
Ted White
Christy M. Whitely
Chris Whitmore
Carol S. Whittaker
John Wike
Danette C. Williams
Frank Wilner
Randolf Win
Mike Winterringer
Adrienne Wisok
Takai Woo
Charlie Woodrow, Capt., USAF
Kim E. Wricht
Mariette Wright
Roy Yanagida
Claire Barrett Young
Karen Zaback
Jeane Zeakus
Anya Zebroski
Joseph Zieglar
Cindy R. Zito
Katie Zoglin

Staff & Photographers

STAFF
David Cohen,
    Editor and Project Director

Susan Wels, Writer
Heather Lindquist,
    Picture Research Director
Peter Howe, Assignment Editor

Jonathan Mills, Production Mgr.
Blanche Brann, Publicity Director
Devyani Kamdar, Finance Mgr.
Teri Stewart, Editorial Coordinator
Noah Rosen, Editorial Assistant

Rick Binger, Rick Binger Design,
    Computer Production
Lucia DeRespinis, Copyeditor
Barry Sundermeier, Fact Checker

William Coblentz, Phillip Feldman
    and E. Gabriel Perle, Attorneys

PICTURE RESEARCHERS
Adrienne Aurichio
Candace Cochrane
Joan Cohen
Mark Dickson
Sandy Ferguson
Stephen L. Hardin
Anne Hobart
George Hobart

PICTURE RESEARCHERS, cont'd.
Cynthia Packard
Barbara Simpson
Timothy Taylor
Laurie Platt Winfrey

NOW PHOTOGRAPHERS
Paul Chesley
Nick Kelsh
Jean-Pierre Laffont
Torin Boyd
Dana Fineman
Ed Lowe
Shelly Katz
Douglas Kirkland
Alice Patterson
Henry Groskinsky
Jamie Thompson
Sebastian Frinzi
Lynn Goldsmith
Dave LaClaire
Ron McQueeney
Jay O'Neil
Joe Rossi
Roger Scruggs

LOGISTICAL ASSISTANCE
Darryl Joyce
Francoise Kirkland
Carole Lee
Kevin Monko

Special thanks to Barbara Loren who helped make this book possible.

THEN & NOW

When Sebastian S. Kresge opened his first store in downtown Detroit in 1899, he gave his turn-of-the-century customers just what they wanted: low prices, attractive product displays and a convenient shopping location. The store's slogan, "Nothing over Ten Cents," was a hit, and by 1912, he had 85 "five and ten" stores with sales over $10 million.

Since then, the company Kresge started has set the pace for retailing in America. Its first Kmart discount department store, opened in 1962, was an instant, record-breaking success. Focusing on value, convenience and customer service, Kmart topped $1 billion in sales in just four years, faster than any other retailer in U.S. history. By the 1970s, more customers were shopping at Kmart stores than at any other chain.

Today, Kmart is still the retailer most consumers know and trust. With its bright new logo, eye-catching displays and inviting, easy-to-shop store design, Kmart is meeting the needs of America's time-, service- and price-conscious shoppers better than ever before.

"Kmart offers all the economies that mass merchandising can produce plus quality that is guaranteed, friendly service where needed and a tradition of integrity."

H.B. Cunningham, President, S.S. Kresge Company
and founder of Kmart discount department stores, 1962

"Kmart, the inventor of the entire discount store industry, has its fingers on the pulse of the consumers of the '90s and the management vision and resources to give them what they want. We are renewed, competitive, successful and in tune with today's consumer."

Joseph E. Antonini, Chairman, President and
Chief Executive Officer, Kmart Corporation, 1991

From the beginning, Kmart has kept pace with American consumers because of the inventiveness and vision of its leaders. In the 1920s, when inflation forced him to raise prices, variety-store pioneer S.S. Kresge kept his customers by opening green-fronted "dollar-or-less" stores next to many of his red-fronted dime-store locations. And in the 1960s, Kresge President H.B. Cunningham took the discount store concept further than anyone in history when he opened the first Kmart discount department store in Garden City, Michigan.

Today, Joseph E. Antonini, Kmart's chairman, president and chief executive officer, is spearheading a bold, $2.5 billion program to renew the entire 2,500-store Kmart chain and keep it in step with changing consumer needs. With an exciting, new store design, improved customer service and finely tuned merchandise, Antonini is ensuring that Kmart will be America's "retailer of choice" well into the 21st century.

Sebastian S. Kresge founded the S.S. Kresge Company in 1899 when he opened his popular five-and-ten variety stores. From 1930 to 1972, the company was headquartered on Second Avenue in Detroit, Michigan.

Over the last 30 years, Kmart stores have been the symbol of successful American retailing. The first Kmarts offered '60s customers low prices, the convenience of store charge accounts and self-service snack bars, plus 40 merchandise departments ranging from men's and boys' wear to major appliances, draperies and auto accessories.

In the 1980s, Kmart boldly updated its apparel program with an exclusive celebrity collection by television star Jaclyn Smith. That successful "signature" approach has been expanded to include high-quality, low-priced bed and bath lines by author Martha Stewart, horticulture advice by "America's master gardener" Jerry Baker, golf clubs by Fuzzy Zoeller and bodywear by world-champion body builder Rachel McLish. Kmart also sponsors the Championship Auto Racing Team headed by world-famous racer Mario Andretti and his son, Michael.

Kmart today is more customer-friendly, attractive and sophisticated than ever. When its expansion and redesign program is completed in 1994, all Kmart stores will feature wide aisles, eye-catching displays and the most popular trend-setting merchandise — as well as low prices, brand-name products, in-store pharmacies and improved customer service. Supporting the stores will be the most advanced computerized data collection and communications system in the industry.

From its earliest beginnings, Kmart has understood and responded to the needs of the American shopper. The new Kmart offers what the new American consumer wants: the best products, the best prices and the best possible shopping experience.

Sixties shoppers loved the variety and low prices of Kmart's new discount department stores.

Today, consumers at this new Kmart store in Sayville, Long Island, enjoy the updated look and exciting fashion displays.

Since 1972, Kmart's international headquarters have been located in Troy, Michigan.

Today, Kmart has grown beyond the boundaries of the discount department store. The Kmart family of companies includes six innovative retailers dedicated to meeting Americans' specialized shopping needs. Waldenbooks, a Kmart division since 1984, is the largest book-store chain in the United States. Builders Square's 150 locations offer consumers building, home-improvement and decorating supplies. The Sports Authority features a wide array of sporting goods and fitness merchandise at everyday low prices. Pay Less Drug Stores have a loyal customer following in 11 western states. PACE is the fourth-largest membership warehouse business in the country. And Office Max, acquired in 1991, is one of the nation's largest office supply superstore chains.

Combined with the power of Kmart stores, these specialty retailers make Kmart part of the daily lifestyle of hundreds of millions of consumers in all 50 states, Canada and Puerto Rico. For Kmart today, more than ever, the watchwords are customer service, shopping ease, quality, low price and great selection.